Transitioning

LEADING YOUR CHURCH THROUGH CHANGE

Dan Southerland

Transitioning

LEADING YOUR CHURCH THROUGH CHANGE

ZondervanPublishingHouse

Grand Rapids, Michigan

A Division of HarperCollinsPublishers

Transitioning
Copyright © 1999 by Dan Southerland
First Zondervan Edition 2000

Requests for information should be addressed to:

🏭 ZondervanPublishingHouse
Grand Rapids, Michigan 49530

Library of Congress Cataloging-in-Publication Data

Southerland, Dan.
    Transitioning: leading your church through change / Dan Southerland.
    p. cm.
    Includes bibliographical references.
    ISBN: 0-310-23344-5 (hardcover)
    1. Church growth. 2. Church renewal. I. Title.
BV652.2 .S59 2000
253-dc 21   96-086314

This edition is printed on acid-free paper.

All Scripture quotations, unless otherwise indicated, are taken from the *Holy Bible: New International Version*®. NIV®. Copyright © 1973, 1978, 1984 by International Bible Society. Used by permission of Zondervan Publishing House. All rights reserved.

Scripture quotations marked NKJ are from *The New King James Bible*, Copyright © 1984.

Scripture quotations marked LB are from *The Living Bible*, Copyright © 1971.

Scripture quotations marked ASV are from *The American Standard Version Bible*, Copyright © 1946.

Printed in the United States of America

00 01 02 03 04 /❖DC/10 9 8 7 6 5 4 3 2 1

Dedication

This book is dedicated to pastors around the world who are leading their churches through transition to become purpose driven. I pray this book guides you.

This book is dedicated to lay leaders around the world who are hungry for what God wants to do in His church. I pray this book encourages you.

This book is dedicated to the millions of unchurched seekers in the world who have quit on church but have not quit on God. I pray this book will enable churches to reach you.

Thanks

Thanks to my family—Mary, Jered, and Danna. You know me best and yet love me most. You are the joy of my life. Thanks to my extended family—Jay and Michelle, whose help means so much. You are the encouragers in my life. Thanks to my church family—who has served as the laboratory for the truths in this book. You are the best church I know. Thanks to the pastors I have the privilege of serving with at Flamingo Road. This is your story as much as it is mine. You are the best of the best. Thanks to Lyman Coleman who made this dream possible. You are a true visionary. Thanks to Jesus Christ from whom all blessings flow. You are the love of my life.

Dedication

Thanks

Table of Contents

Foreword

Since the publication of *The Purpose-Driven® Church* in 1995, over 500,000 church leaders from around the world have been introduced to the principles of building a healthy church based on the foundation of Christ's Great Commandment and Great Commission. Today, tens of thousands of churches are transitioning from being program driven to being purpose driven. An incredible wave of renewal and revival is taking place in these churches that are willing to change.

One of the most exciting and encouraging examples of that is happening at Flamingo Road Church in Fort Lauderdale, Florida, under the dynamic leadership of Pastor Dan Southerland. Dan is a wise, seasoned leader. He has led his congregation to renewal, health, and amazing growth through a brilliant step-by-step process of transitioning.

As a result, his church has grown from around 300 in attendance to well over 2,000! Even more exciting is the fact that over 60 percent of the people they reach today are unchurched. This is not a church that has grown at the expense of other churches. In fact, while his congregation has been growing, it has been instrumental in planting 16 other churches.

Being purpose driven has nothing to do with your denomination, worship style, evangelistic target, size, or location. The essence of the purpose driven paradigm is a simple, biblical strategy and structure that insures equal emphasis is given to all five New Testament purposes of the church. Most churches tend to overemphasize one of the purposes (evangelism, discipleship, worship, ministry, or fellowship) to the neglect of the others. This always creates imbalance. But, as Dan Southerland's wonderful story illustrates, balance creates health. And when a church is healthy, growth occurs naturally and automatically.

This is a book to be studied, not just read. To get the most out of it I encourage you to purchase a copy for each of your staff and study it together, one chapter at a time, as many have already done with *The Purpose-Driven® Church*. Discuss the implications of each chapter for your church and create a list of action steps you intend to take.

As we move into the twenty-first century, I believe the greatest days of the church are all ahead of us and I firmly believe there is hope for our older established churches who will take the risk of rediscovering God's purpose for the church.

If you are a pastor or key leader in an established church—this manual will help you implement the principles of being purpose driven. So go for it! My prayer is that God will use this book to enable you, as He did King David, to "serve God's purpose in your generation" (Acts 13:36).

Rick Warren
Author of *The Purpose-Driven® Church*

The Flamingo Road Story

In the fall of 1989, Flamingo Road Church in Fort Lauderdale, Florida, was at a crossroads. This traditional church of 300 in worship had just experienced its second stretch of being without a pastor or staff in three years. In desperation, the church hired three men within a month—and began what has become the ride of a lifetime!

Flamingo Road experienced solid growth over the next several months. By the spring of 1990, we were well on our way to becoming a large, traditional church. But we made a discovery that was heart breaking: we were not reaching unchurched, lost people. Our growth was 90 percent transfers from churches and only 10 percent by winning people to Christ.

That began our journey of discovering how to do church for the unchurched. We went to school on many different churches that were reaching unchurched people. The church that influenced us most was Saddleback Church of Mission Viejo, California. We came to realize that a common sense approach to purpose, target, and strategy was what we needed to apply in our own setting.

After a year of studying, seeking, and praying, we set out to make the transition. God has blessed us in an amazing way. In reality, there are nine specific transitions we have made:

- **approach** – from program driven to purpose driven
- **target** – from reaching "fellow Baptists" to reaching the unchurched
- **worship style** – from traditional to extremely contemporary
- **leadership** – from a committee / deacon-led church to a staff-led church
- **pastors** – from a senior pastor model to multiple pastors
- **ministry** – from staff doing all the ministry to staff being the equippers and lay ministers doing the ministry
- **strategy** – from no systematic plan for reaching the lost and developing those we win to a life cycle process that is driven by small groups
- **schedule** – from worship on Sunday morning only to two services Saturday night and two on Sunday morning
- **small groups** – from traditional Sunday school to relational small groups

These transitions have not been easy or immediate—but they have been effective. We have grown from a church of 300 in attendance in the fall of 1989 to a total of 2100 today. We have started sixteen missions and grand missions that now average another 3000 in worship attendance. And we are now reaching unchurched people: about 60 percent of those who join us today are unchurched before they come to Flamingo Road.

We are more aware than ever that God is not finished with us. We are ahead of schedule to reach the goals we set years ago of 2000 in worship by the year 2000 and 10,000 by the year 2010. One burden we share is to help other churches and pastors to make these transitions. We believe you can learn from the experience of others, and our heart is to make our experiences available to any who can benefit from them.

Introduction

Why a book on transitioning?

Travis and Garrett are each given a block of wood and a knife. Both boys immediately begin whittling. Both are working hard. Both are serious about their work. Both are enjoying the task.

When they are finished, the two boys have quite different results. Travis has carved a boat. Garrett has whittled his wood away into a pile of shavings.

What was different about the two boys? Travis had vision—which meant he could see the end result. He also understood transition—how to get from where he was to where he wanted to go. He had a purpose, a target, and a strategy. Garrett—while working equally hard—was just whittling.

Why do we need a book on transitioning to a purpose driven church? Because many, if not most, of our churches are just whittling. According to recent studies, 80 percent of churches in North America are plateaued or in decline. On the edge of the twenty-first century, with opportunities that are unparalleled in

Christian history, we are whittling away while the world goes to hell in a handbasket.

On the positive side, the church as a whole does care about people. The church is working hard to show the world that we love God. The difficulty is not a heart issue. The issue is much more subtle than that. We have lost our vision. In the twenty centuries since Jesus first handed us the keys to the kingdom, we have lost our way.

In an effort to regain that vision, hundreds of thousands of church leaders have attended conferences in the past decade on leadership, vision, and purpose. They go home fired up about what can happen in their churches. But they all face the same struggle: How do we transition the church from where we are to where we want to go?

Why now?

God is doing something fresh in the world today. The largest churches in the history of Christianity are being built, including multiple churches in South America and Korea that have more than 100,000 people in regular attendance. Whole continents are seeing revival. According to Open Doors International, 10,000 people a day are coming to faith in South America and 30,000 a day in Africa.

We are on the edge of a second reformation. The first reformation of the 1500s and 1600s was about the message, about returning to what the Bible really says about sin and salvation, about how we relate to God. In the first reformation, the Bible was given back to the people.

The second reformation is about methods. It concerns how

we should relate to the world around us; how we make the gospel culturally relevant so that men and women everywhere can come to know, love, and serve Jesus Christ. In this second reformation, the ministry of the church is being given back to the people.

Why are you reading this book?

How do we transition the church back to a purpose driven model? How do we lead the church back to the Biblical principles of being culturally relevant without being culturally compromised? How do we reform the way we do church to a contemporary and purpose driven model so that the timeless message of salvation in Christ can be received and understood by those we so desperately want to reach?

If these and other related questions are keeping you up at night, this book is for you. There seems to be a growing hunger among church leaders to understand transition and to be able to lead it in the local church. This book is written for such leaders.

If you are happy with how the church is doing, this book is not for you. But if you are desperate to see revival, hungry to see seekers come to Christ, and ready to see the church become a force in your community like never before, read on.

This is not a book about why the church needs to transition. If you need to be convinced of that, you will be frustrated here. This is a book about how to lead transition in the church. It is written for those who are already convinced that change must occur. It is for those who long to lead their churches to become purpose driven but don't know how to go about it.

Why am I writing this book?

I have had the privilege of being one of the pastors of a church that has successfully navigated the waters of transition. Nine years ago, Flamingo Road Church was a traditional, program driven church that was dead in the water in terms of growth. In the past nine years, we have made nine major transitions, grown sevenfold in attendance, and started sixteen other mission churches. Today we are a fully contemporary, fully transitioned, fully purpose driven church. It has been the ride of a life time—and I truly believe we are just getting started.

I am convinced that God allowed us to learn about transition so that we could share it with other church leaders. The book that follows is the compilation of what we have learned along the way. It is by no means a final word on the subject of transition. We need many more such books. But before we can have many, there must be a first. To my knowledge, this is the first book to deal with leading transition in the church as a process.

My hope is that what follows will be used of God to help you lead your church through whatever transitional crossroads it is facing. My prayer is that you will be stretched, challenged, and encouraged to lead transition in a brand new way. If that occurs, then the church will transition to become truly purpose driven.

Overview

Some high school teacher, whose name has long since escaped me, taught me a rule of communication many years ago. Her suggestion was to follow this format: tell them what you are going to tell them, tell them, and then tell them what you told them. In easier terms: overview, view, and review. So this is the "here is what I hope to cover" section.

This book is organized around a process of vision. It is taken from the book of Nehemiah. In rebuilding the wall, Nehemiah followed an eight-step process of vision. That same process is presented here.

Step one is *Preparing for Vision*. Before we can receive God's vision we must prepare for it. I am personally convinced that this is the most overlooked step in the vision process. When it is followed, the stage is set for vision in a God-honoring way. When it is ignored or omitted, the stage is set for disaster. Don't leave step one until you fully grasp it. Even those readers who have a fully defined vision may discover some steps of preparation that need further attention.

Step two will deal with *Defining the Vision*. Nothing can

become dynamic until it becomes specific. There are three specific questions that every church must answer: What is our purpose? Who is our target? What is our strategy? The answers to those three questions will together form the vision of the church. Preparing for vision is the most foundational part of the vision process; but defining vision is the most crucial and controversial area. Many churches die in the midst of this second step. For those church leaders who have not yet defined vision, this chapter is essential. Those who have a defined vision in place will still benefit from a review.

Step three begins the actual transition process by focusing on *Planting the Vision*. Vision is a living seed. Before it can grow in the life of the church it must be planted in the hearts of church leaders. This step deals with how to strategically bring key leaders on board with the vision to the place where it is a vision they share rather than a vision they oppose.

Step four addresses the issue of *Sharing the Vision* with the remainder of the church. Every visionary wants his vision to be caught by the entire church. Since vision is both caught and taught, it must be shared in multiple ways to be effectively communicated.

Step five in the vision process is *Implementing the Vision*. In this step, the change process begins. Now is the time to decide several important issues: what changes need to be made, what order of change, what role do church leaders play in the change process, and where do you put people to work?

Step six is *Dealing with Opposition*. This may be the number one dropout point in the vision process. All leaders experience opposition. Knowing what to expect and learning how to stay on track is vital.

Step seven focuses on *Making Course Corrections*. Every visionary must learn to make adjustments on the fly. Nehemiah had to make three specific course corrections in the middle of his project. Church leaders today should expect no less.

Step eight details the process for *Evaluating the Results*. When vision is complete, there are eight specific and obvious evidences that are present. These can be used as measuring sticks for any transition.

The last chapter is entitled *Concluding Thoughts*. It is a brief statement of five realities concerning the process of vision that will encourage any leader to stay actively involved in transition.

Step 1

Preparing For Vision

In my family, we grew up with a standard vacation plan. Every year we would drive from whatever part of Texas or Oklahoma we were living in at the time to the same lake in Arkansas where we would go tent camping. And we would spend every waking moment skiing, swimming, fishing, and motorcycling.

Taking a family of six on a two week out-in-the-woods style vacation was not a small venture. Although the journey to our destination was not long (five–six hours), it took weeks of getting ready. It was such a major change in lifestyle to transition from the suburbs to the lake shore that it took some very deliberate preparation to pull it off.

Vision is not just a destination; it is a journey

Preparation is a major part of vision. The reason lies in the essence of vision itself. Vision is not just a destination; it is a journey. Vision is not just a product; it is a process. Vision is not just the finish line; it is the whole race.

Any business guru can tell you that research and development is a major part of producing a winning product. Any athlete knows that winning the competition begins with training. Any seasoned traveler can testify that front end preparation is vital to a successful trip.

> **Vision is not just the finish line; it is the whole race.**

Paul captured the essence of vision when he wrote these words:

> *"No eye has seen, no ear has heard, no mind has conceived what God has prepared for those who love him."*
>
> *1 Corinthians 2:9*

For our eyes to see God's vision, for our ears to hear God's voice, and for our minds to conceive of God's plan, we must spend time in major preparation. Before we can receive God's vision for His church we must prepare for vision. God's vision for your church is big stuff so the preparation for that vision must be big stuff as well.

Our plans versus God's vision

I love this verse about vision:

> *Many are the plans in a man's heart, but it is the Lord's purpose that prevails.* *Proverbs 19:21*

This verse was written with today's church in mind. Today, our churches tend to have many plans. They have numerous programs and multifaceted ministries. Never before in history has the church tried to offer so much.

Yet I wonder if most of our churches have discovered God's vision. Have they found the *"purpose that prevails"*—which is God's purpose? I believe that the numerous plans that we come up with won't get the job done. Only God's plan will prevail.

What is vision?

Henry Blackaby's study, *Experiencing God*, is nothing short of life changing for those who have been through it. The essence of Blackaby's work can be boiled down to one idea: see what God is doing and join Him. Rather than asking God to bless our plan and our vision, we must see what God is doing around us and join God in His plan and His vision.

What is vision? Vision is a picture of what God wants to do. Vision is a picture of what God will do in His church if we get out of His way and turn Him loose to do it. So the process of vision is the process of joining God in what He is doing and wants to do in His church.

Vision is a picture of what God wants to do.

As a junior in high school, I was part of a youth mission trip to a small church in Idaho. When we arrived, the girls were taken to homes for lodging while the boys set up quarters in the church building. The only problem with this arrangement was the lack of a place for the boys to shower and clean up. After a few days this problem was becoming apparent to anyone within several hundred yards of the boys. So our youth pastor asked the pastor of the host church where the boys could clean up. He informed us that just beyond the tree line at the edge of the church property was a beautiful, crystal clear river that flowed straight down from the mountains and that we were welcome to bathe there.

That discovery changed the entire trip. Every day thereafter the boys would spend a few minutes of much needed fun and refreshment (and odor improvement) in that river.

I have thought often about that river over the years. I am convinced of this truth: the river of what God wants to do is flowing nearby every one of our churches if we will just discover it and get immersed in it. God has a river of vision for each of His churches—and most of us are not even aware it is there.

> **The seven last words of a dying church: "We never did it that way before."**

Vision is an active process, an ongoing process. It is a continual search for what God is doing and wants to do.

> *Therefore, if anyone is in Christ, he is a new creation; old things have passed away; behold, all things have become new.*
> 2 Corinthians 5:17 (NKJ)

Unfortunately, in many of our churches, we have changed that verse to read like this:

> *Therefore, if anyone is in Christ, he is an old creation; new things have passed away; behold, all things have become old.*
> (Modern Church Perversion)

This translation would be especially liked in those churches who cling to the seven last words of a dying church: "We never did it that way before." But churches who are vision driven are more attached to a present tense version of this verse:

Therefore, if anyone stays in Christ, he is a renewed creation; old things keep passing away, and all things keep becoming new.

That is vision. Vision is the active process of following a dynamic God—which means we must keep dreaming and keep visioning to keep our churches, ministries, and personal lives from perishing.

> We must keep dreaming and keep visioning to keep our churches, ministries, and personal lives from perishing.

The art of spiritual surfing

One of the finest books ever written about vision and purpose is Rick Warren's book *The Purpose Driven Church*. Rick opens his book with an analogy about spiritual surfing. Spiritual surfing has three parts:

- **See the wave** of what God is doing. God is at work in the world today in major ways. You must first see what God is up to and wants to do in your community.

  Have you seen those pictures within a picture? The kind you must stare at for a while before you can see the real but hidden image? Vision is the same idea. Anyone can see the obvious stuff. But what is God doing behind the scenes?

- **Catch the wave** of what God is doing. After you spot the wave you must catch it. That in itself is no small feat. It takes timing, courage, and skill. It also requires risk taking —because you must leave the safety of the shore to catch the biggest waves.

- **Ride the wave** of what God is doing. A lot of surfers can get up on a wave. The goal is to stay up and surf the wave as far and as long as you can. You don't want to abandon the wave; you want to ride it out all the way.

The importance of preparation

Follow this logic with me for a moment:

- If vision is a picture of what God wants to do in His church
- And if the key to vision is joining God in what He wants to do in His church
- And if God wants to give us His vision
- Then when we are prepared for vision, God gives it to us!

So the question is "What are the steps of preparation?" That is a great question.

Nehemiah: A study in vision

> The question is: "What are the steps of preparation?"

The process of vision upon which this book is based comes from the Old Testament book of Nehemiah. Why Nehemiah? Two major reasons. First, Nehemiah was one of the most visionary leaders of the Bible. He pulled off a project that is one of the most amazing in all of Scripture—the rebuilding of the wall around Jerusalem. Second, the book of Nehemiah contains the step-by-step process of vision. In the steps that Nehemiah followed, we find the steps we need to follow in order to lead our churches through transition.

In Nehemiah chapter one, we find five steps of preparation for vision.

1. Collect information   Study

Notice how Nehemiah opens his book:

> *The words of Nehemiah son of Hacaliah: In the month of Kislev in the twentieth year, while I was in the citadel of Susa, Hanani, one of my brothers, came from Judah with some other men, and* **I questioned them about the Jewish remnant that survived the exile, and also about Jerusalem.** *They said to me, "Those who survived the exile and are back in the province are in great trouble and disgrace. The wall of Jerusalem is broken down, and its gates have been burned with fire."*
>
> Nehemiah 1:1–3

Nehemiah questioned those with firsthand experience about the conditions in Jerusalem. He gathered all the information he could. He studied the circumstance. Why would he do this? Because Nehemiah understood this vital principle: vision is best birthed out of thorough knowledge. Contrary to what some people believe, it is not unspiritual to think. Or to study. Or to do some basic research. In other words, it is OK to use your brain. Thinking is actually allowed.

> **Vision is best birthed out of thorough knowledge.**

Time to go to school

There are two areas where we must go to school in order to collect the necessary information to prepare for vision.

First, go to school on *the unchurched people in your community*. From time to time, I will hear some well-intentioned preacher say, "All we need to do is preach the word of God." That

> **We need to understand the people we are trying to reach.**

statement is not true. The preaching of the Word is central and is fundamental. We must in fact have Biblical preaching for people to come to know Jesus Christ. But if good preaching alone would win the world to Christ, we would have finished the job long ago. We also need to understand the people we are trying to reach.

Paul—one of the main visionaries of the early church— said:

> *Though I am free and belong to no man, I make myself a slave to everyone, to win as many as possible. To the Jews I became like a Jew, to win the Jews. To those under the law I became like one under the law (though I myself am not under the law), so as to win those under the law. To those not having the law I became like one not having the law (though I am not free from God's law but am under Christ's law), so as to win those not having the law. To the weak I became weak, to win the weak.* **I have become all things to all men so that by all possible means I might save some. I do all this for the sake of the gospel.**   *1 Corinthians 9:19–23*

How did Paul know what it would take to win the Jews? Or to reach those under the law? Or to relate to those who did not have the law or to the weak? He studied them. He collected all the information he could about those he was trying to reach.

I spent thirteen years of my life in youth ministry. During those years I observed that some youth pastors were really effective in reaching teenagers while others were not. One of the characteristics of those who were effective was an understanding of adolescence. Those who understood teens did not expect them to behave as adults—but neither did they treat them like children. They customized their ministry to meet the needs of the group they were trying to reach.

Do not make the mistake of thinking you know the unchurched people in your community. Chances are you might be surprised at what you find if you take the time to do the research.

The second area we must go to school on *is churches that are reaching unchurched people*. When we began studying how to reach the unchurched people in our community at Flamingo Road Church, we went to school on those churches in our country that were reaching large numbers of unchurched people. Our list included First Baptist Church of Jacksonville, Willow Creek Community in Chicago, Saddleback Church in South Orange County, Eastside Foursquare Church in Seattle and Wooddale Church in Minneapolis.

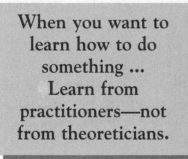

When you want to learn how to do something ... Learn from practitioners—not from theoreticians.

When you want to learn how to do something, go to school on the folks who have proven they know how to do it because they are doing it. Learn from practitioners—not from theoreticians. Many claim to know how to do it. Those who really know how to do it are doing it.

Collecting information is the first step of preparation for vision because you need to understand the people you are trying to reach.

Evaluate

2. Holy discontent with the status quo

What Nehemiah learned about the conditions in Jerusalem changed Nehemiah's heart forever. Check out his response to the information he received:

> *When I heard these things, I sat down and wept.*
> *Nehemiah 1:4a*

Nehemiah was heartbroken. The walls had been down for years, but all of a sudden he experiences a holy discontent with that fact. God gave him a bad case of holy heartache. God broke his heart over the people of Jerusalem and their desolate condition. God let Nehemiah feel about Jerusalem the way that He felt about Jerusalem. God let Nehemiah see Jerusalem the way He saw Jerusalem.

As long as we are content with the status quo, we will not discover God's vision.

Don't miss this major principle of transitioning: vision is usually birthed out of heartache and burden. It must come from the heart.

How many times does the Bible tell us that:

- Jesus wept over the lost sheep of Israel (Matthew 10:6).
- Moses stood in the gap for the Israelites (Exodus 17:4).
- Jeremiah wept over the burden he carried (Jeremiah 3:21).

As long as we are content with the status quo, we will not discover God's vision.

I had the privilege of teaching this material not long ago in the state of Missouri. Just before we were about to start the conference, I met a local pastor. When I asked him how things were going in his church, he replied, "Well, things are comfortable." To this pastor's credit, he came up after the conference and said, "That was the wrong answer, wasn't it?"

As long as we are comfortable with the way things are, we cannot receive God's vision. As long as we are happy with the status quo, God won't speak. If we are more concerned about not rocking the boat than we are with storming the gates of hell, we will never discover God's plan and power in our churches.

Vision often comes in times of desperation

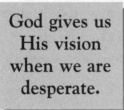

God gives us His vision when we are desperate.

Some of you are reading this book because you are desperate. I want to congratulate you. That is a good thing. You will receive more from this book than those who are content with what is happening in their churches.

God gives us His vision when we are desperate. He speaks to us when our whole heart and mind and soul is set on Him. When we are really hungry and thirsty for God, we find Him. Jesus said it this way: *"Blessed are those who hunger and thirst for righteousness, for they shall be satisfied"* (Matthew 5:6, NAS).

The point of desperation came for us at Flamingo Road Church in the spring of 1990. There were four of us on the pastoral staff at that time. We had been at the church six months. During that six months, the church had grown in worship attendance from 300 to 500—which was pretty impressive. In fact, we were pretty impressed with ourselves.

We went away on a staff retreat to pat ourselves on the back. But while we were on that retreat, we did some analysis of our growth and made a life changing discovery. We learned that 90 percent of our growth were transfers from other area churches. Only 10 percent of our growth came from people we were winning to Christ. We were growing by swapping sheep! Our church had simply become the hottest church in town and every Christian who was unhappy or disgruntled in the least with their church was joining ours.

I cannot describe adequately the heartbreak that settled into our souls at that moment. We went from being as high as a kite about our growth to being broken and desperate. We made a commitment to learn to do church for the unchurched —and we have been learning ever since.

I am convinced that a major reason we do not discover God's vision for our churches is that we are content with business as usual. Vision must be fueled by a holy discontent with the status quo.

3. Fasting

Nehemiah had just received the devastating news about the conditions in Jerusalem. What was his next response?

> *For some days I mourned and fasted and prayed before the God of heaven.*   *Nehemiah 1:4b*

Nehemiah fasted for several days. Although fasting was practiced throughout the Old Testament and New Testament times, it is almost nonexistent in many churches today. In the Old Testament, fasting was practiced in four ways: as a way to humble yourself (Ezra 8:21), as a form of confession

(1 Samuel 7:6), as a sign of repentance (Jonah 3:5–8), and as a form of prayer (Daniel 9:3). In the New Testament, fasting is seen as a part of serious prayer (Acts 14:23) and is assumed to be a normal part of the Christian life (Matthew 6:16; 9:15). Jesus fasted regularly—including a forty day fast at the start of his ministry (Matthew 4:2) and shorter fasts before major ministry events.

What is fasting?

Many church leaders today know little or nothing about fasting even though it is clearly a scriptural process. It is a definite part of preparing for vision.

My definition of fasting: fasting is giving up food or some other activity in order to devote more serious time and attention to prayer.

Essentially, there are two parts to fasting: a giving up and an adding to. You give up something regular in your schedule. The general standard is to give up food, but fasting can mean giving up any identified activity. (Some of us might benefit greatly from a little less TV.)

But fasting is not just a giving up—it is also an adding to. When you fast, you give up something in order to do more of something else. Fasting is adding more time and energy to spend in prayer. In fact, fasting is as serious a form of prayer as we have. It is a method of seeking God that we dare not overlook.

Why fast?

Why should we fast? And how is fasting related to vision? Vision is usually birthed out of a serious search for God's direction. It is amazing how many times we claim we are seriously searching for God's plan when we have not fasted to seek God. Most of us have spent far more time going to school on what is

Vision is usually birthed out of a serious search for God's direction.

working in other churches than we have spent seeking God for what He wants to do in our church.

You don't find vision when you search for vision. You find God's vision when you search for God. Fasting is a serious part of that search.

One of my first experiences with fasting and vision came in late 1991. The pastors on the staff had spent over a year praying, seeking, studying, and talking about vision. We were about to start making some plans for transition at the church. I went away with a Bible and a legal pad for a three-day retreat —just me and God. This is a hard thing for me to do because I am a party animal who does not like being alone. But I was not alone. During that three days of fasting and praying, God showed up and assured me that it was time to go for it. We have been going for it ever since.

Do not underestimate the importance of fasting. I do not believe you can say with integrity that you have sought God's vision for your church until you have sought Him in times of fasting.

4. Prayer

Nehemiah had a commitment that is sadly missing in many church leaders today: a major commitment to prayer. He understood the relationship between prayer and vision.

Notice the depth of his commitment:

> *Then I said: "O Lord, God of heaven, the great and awesome*
> *God, who keeps his covenant of love with those who love him*
> *and obey his commands, let your ear be attentive and your eyes*
> *open to hear the prayer your servant is **praying before you***
> ***day and night** for your servants, the people of Israel. I con-*
> *fess the sins we Israelites, including myself and my father's*
> *house, have committed against you."*   Nehemiah 1:5–6

Nehemiah fasted for several days—but he prayed for several
months. He bathed his vision in prayer from start to finish.
Notice how he ended his prayer:

> *"O Lord, let your ear be attentive to the prayer of this your ser-*
> *vant and to the prayer of your servants who delight in revering*
> *your name. Give your servant success today by granting him*
> *favor in the presence of this man."*   Nehemiah 1:11

Having trouble hearing God?

One problem we have with receiving God's vision is hearing
God's voice. We are often so busy serving God that we have
trouble being still enough to hear His voice.

King David recognized that there is a set order when it comes
to the relationship of prayer and vision:

> *"Be still, and know that I am God; I will be exalted among the*
> *nations, I will be exalted in the earth."*   Psalm 46:10

Don't miss that order. First, I must be still enough to hear God.
Second, I will be able to know Him and what He wants me to
do. Third, God will be exalted as His vision is carried out.

Many times church leaders suffer from the Elijah syndrome. Elijah had followed God long enough to see God do some pretty incredible things (food a la raven, flour that never is used up, raising the widow's son from the dead, stopping the rain for three and a half years, calling down fire on the false prophets, and other minor stuff like this—see 1 Kings 17–18). But Elijah got so busy working for God that he did not make time to seek God. Soon the same leader who had been used in such big ways for God was running from a vengeful woman. When Elijah again seeks God, God speaks to him—but not through the big and dramatic. He speaks to Elijah in a gentle whisper (1 Kings 19).

Those who talk with God most usually hear God best.

That is the Elijah syndrome—being so busy doing big things for God that we do not take the time to seek God. The problem with not spending time in prayer is simply this: those who talk with God most usually hear God best. And those who do not talk to God often usually do not hear Him at all. The number one hindrance to answered prayer for many church leaders today is prayerlessness. We just don't pray.

The relationship between vision and prayer

One of my favorite passages on prayer and vision is found in Jeremiah 29:11–13. Notice the progression of the promise that is found in those verses.

> *"For I know the plans I have for you," declares the Lord, "plans to prosper you and not to harm you, plans to give you hope and a future."*   Jeremiah 29:11

That sounds a lot like vision, doesn't it? God has a plan. And it is a good plan. It is a plan to prosper His people. His plan is not to be feared but will give us hope and a solid future.

How do we find that plan? The next verse tells us.

> *"Then you will call upon me and come and pray to me, and I will listen to you."*   Jeremiah 29:12

Many of the promises in the Bible have a condition. The promised vision of verse 11 is based on the condition of verse 12—that we pray. In fact, the verse tells us three times that we are to pray—*"call upon me* and *come* and *pray to me."*

The following verse gives us the details of the condition:

> *"You will seek me and find me when you seek me with all your heart."*   Jeremiah 29:13

If you want to find all of God's vision you must seek Him with all of your heart.

Who finds God's vision?

Vision is usually given to those who pray until they get it. If prayer is not the octane that fuels your vision, your vision will stall out and your church will be motionless.

> **Vision is usually given to those who pray until they get it.**

Every church leader depends on something for their main resource. For some, it is personality; for others, knowledge; still others depend on past experience. We often run off the strength of that main source until we come to the end of our-selves and cry out to God.

What are you depending on God to do? The answer is rather easy to discover. Those things you are praying for are the things you are depending on God to do. Those things you are not praying for, you are doing on your own.

You cannot do vision on your own. Prayer is a major prerequi-site. If you want to test your commitment to praying for vision, do this exercise. Rate yourself from 1 to 100 on pray-ing for vision. Write a number down based on how much you have prayed for vision in the last year. Now put a percent sign after that number. And know this: that is the maximum per-cent of God's vision you can receive for your church.

There is no shortcut to vision. We must pray if we want to know God's vision for His church—because God gives vision to people of prayer.

5. Waiting   *what on God*

Notice the behind the scenes waiting going on in Nehemiah's vision process. First, the wall in Jerusalem had been down for seventy years. Second, Nehemiah had been in the king's ser-vice for twenty years. There is some major waiting taking place here. And even after Nehemiah got started in his vision quest, he had a four month time lapse. Chapter one of Nehemiah occurs in "Kislev" (see Nehemiah 1:1), which is the Persian name for December. Chapter two of Nehemiah occurs in "Nisan" (see Nehemiah 2:1) which sounds like a for-eign automobile but is actually the Persian name for April. What did Nehemiah do during this four month time lapse between chapters one and two? He waited!

Vision is usually given to those who patiently wait for it

I hate to wait. Some days it seems that my entire life is on hold. The line I choose at the bank inevitably shuts down. The lady in front of me in the grocery store checkout line always needs a price check. The doctor's office is always full of sick people (funny how that works).

The problem is that we hate to wait. We live in an instant nation. We have instant coffee (that tastes and smells just like the real thing to me). We have instant potatoes (that are a lot quicker and easier than the real thing). We have a microwave mentality (if we can figure out which buttons to push to run the darn thing).

Even the people in our churches think they can have instant maturity. They want to go from being a total mess one day to being Billy Graham the next.

> **Waiting is a big part of preparing for vision.**

We do the same thing as church leaders. We want to go from asking God for vision one day to having every detail worked out the next. Few of us like to wait. But waiting is a big part of preparing for vision. In fact, vision is usually given to those who patiently wait for it.

> *But those who wait on the Lord shall renew their strength; they shall mount up with wings like eagles, they shall run and not be weary, they shall walk and not faint.*
>
> Isaiah 40:31 (NKJ)

Waiting and God's will

I have spent all of my life in church. As I grew up, I heard many speak of "God's will" and yet I never fully understood what that meant.

Here is a working definition of God's will.

- doing the right *thing*
- in the right *way*
- for the right *motive*
- at the right *time*

> **The difference in a home run and a long foul ball is timing.**

Notice the importance of waiting. The difference in a home run and a long foul ball is timing. Sometimes we have to wait—even though we hate doing it.

Wrap up

At the end of each transition step, I will give you a key concept (or sometimes two) to remember.

Key Truth: Rushed preparation results in sloppy vision.

There is some tough homework to be done in the school of vision. You must collect information about your community. You must develop a holy discontent with the status quo in your church. You must fast and pray in order to seek God. And you must wait, and wait, and wait....

Flamingo Road Church has been through more deliberate, planned transition than any church I know of anywhere. A list of some of the major transitions we have made over the past nine years would include:

- **approach** – from program driven to purpose driven
- **target** – from Christians to the unchurched
- **worship** – from traditional to extremely contemporary
- **leadership** – from committee/deacon led to staff led
- **pastors** – from a senior pastor model to multiple pastors
- **ministry** – from staff doing all the ministry to staff being the equippers and lay ministers doing the ministry
- **strategy** – from no systematic plan for reaching the lost and developing those we win to a life cycle process that is driven by small groups
- **schedule** – from Sunday morning only to two services on Saturday night and two on Sunday morning
- **small groups** – from a traditional Sunday school plan to a relational, participation-oriented small group approach
- **missions** – from no plan for starting mission churches to sixteen mission church starts
- **size** – from 300 to 2100 in worship attendance with another 3000 in worship attendance in our missions

Any one of these transitions could have destroyed the church. Examples of derailings over these and other transitions are plentiful. None of these transitions could have occurred if we had not been willing to do the necessary steps of preparation.

If you are not willing to do the homework, don't lead the church to change. Rushed preparation results in sloppy vision.

> **Rushed preparation results in sloppy vision.**

Too many times church leaders (especially us pastor types) attend a conference or hear about a church or get an idea from somewhere else and rush to make changes in the church accordingly. The result is that our churches are forced to go through the trauma and shock of a rushed transition. You must take the time to do the hard homework of preparation. Otherwise you will flunk the test of being able to lead your church through transition.

You must go slow if you want to stay long

If you are on your way to another ministry, don't you dare make changes. If you are not willing to stay, don't lead the church to make transitions. If you are not willing to go slow, don't change.

Doug Murren pastored the Eastside Foursquare Church in Seattle for many years. He also wrote

> "The reason 99 out of 100 churches that try to make major transitions fail is that they go too fast."

BabyBoomerang—an excellent book on reaching unchurched young adults. Doug once told me, "The reason 99 out of 100 churches that try to make major transitions fail is that they go too fast." I could not agree more!

Our transitions here at Flamingo Road were deliberately done slowly. We took four years to make them. Some church leaders tell me "I don't have four years." I respond by telling them that I have made a public commitment to stay at Flamingo Road Church for twenty years. I want to give the best twenty years of my life to one place. When you have made a twenty year commitment, taking four years to transition is no big deal. In fact, four years of slow transition for sixteen years of doing church purpose driven style is a great swap. If that seems a long time to wait, you might remember that Jesus took thirty years to prepare for a three year ministry.

Time spent in deliberate preparation is never wasted time. Taking the time to build a solid foundation is crucial. The foundation is always important because it determines the stability of the structure that is built upon it. Jesus taught us that the wise among us pay attention to the foundation we build upon (Matthew 7:24–27).

If you rush the preparation process for vision, you will end up with a shaky foundation. Chances are that your vision will not stand when the storms come against it.

Step one—you must prepare for vision.

Step 2

Defining the Vision

All great leaders are willing to ask tough questions. They believe curiosity is a virtue. One of the requirements for taking new territory is the ability to question the status quo.

The first step in the vision process requires some serious preparation. This second step requires some serious question asking—and more importantly, finding some answers.

When we left Nehemiah he was preparing for vision. That is the first step in the process and it is detailed in Nehemiah chapter one. But something dramatic happens to Nehemiah in the four month time lapse between chapters one and two. In chapter one he is burdened about Jerusalem but has no specific plan. In chapter two he has the plan firmly in place. What happened in between? He moved from preparing for vision to defining a very specific vision.

You must do the same. To lead your church to be purpose driven, you must discover God's specific vision for your church.

When God leads us He gives us specific leadership

From the statements that we hear in our churches, we seem to believe that God gives us specific leadership. We say "God led me to this church" when discussing how we got here. I often hear phrases like "God has been putting you on my heart" when we talk about the people we are holding up in prayer. I even hear statements like "God led me to marry that girl" (although it is usually from newly-weds). We believe that God gives us very specific leadership.

I believe that God wants to give every one of his churches very specific leadership in the area of vision. Those specifics would include *what* He wants us to do, *when* He wants us to do it, and *how* He wants us to

> God wants to give every one of his churches very specific leadership in the area of vision.

get the job done. You cannot become a purpose driven church until you answer these three crucial questions.

Three steps to defining vision

Peter Drucker has been called the father of modern American management. He is certainly a recognized authority in today's business world. Drucker is probably best known for the two questions he most often uses. The first is "What business are we in?" And the second is "How's business?"

In terms of the church's effort to define vision, I would suggest a three part adaptation of Drucker's questions. What business are we in? Who is our primary customer? How will we reach that customer?

There are three steps that every church must take in order to define God's vision. They have to do with purpose, target, and strategy. Rick Warren's book *The Purpose Driven Church* is the most thorough treatment available concerning purpose, target, and strategy. I believe Rick is one of God's special gifts to this generation. I highly recommend his book. Much of my understanding (and my material) concerning purpose, target, and strategy come from him. For those who have read Rick's book, this chapter will serve as a review. For those who have not read *The Purpose Driven Church*, this chapter is essential.

1. Discover your purpose

Vini, vidi, vici. That is all I remember from Latin class (we did have a really cool toga party). I will never know as long as I live why I needed to spend two years of junior high school studying Latin. The first day the teacher gave us her version of the purpose of studying Latin, which went something like this: "Latin is

> **Three steps to defining vision:**
>
> 1. **Discover your purpose**
> 2. **Define your target**
> 3. **Decide your strategy**

a dead language that is no longer spoken anyplace in the world. But it is a classic language that should never die. That is why we are studying Latin."

That made no sense to me at all. The reason for studying a dead language was to keep it from dying? To keep it on artificial life support? That was the purpose?

Many churches today are dealing with a similar struggle. They are yet to discover why they are doing what they do. If they do not make that discovery, they are in fact in danger of becoming dying institutions whose only purpose is survival. Even some of our church signs point out that we think our purpose is survival. They declare "established in 1882"—as if we are proud of the fact that we are still in existence.

Jesus said something a bit different about His vision for the church:

> *"I will build my church; and all the powers of hell shall not prevail against it."*   Matthew 16:18 (TLB)

That sounds like more than survival to me. That sounds like a church that is driven by purpose.

Purpose is the first and biggest issue of vision. The major question that must be answered here is *what does God want us to do.* In other words, what business are we in?

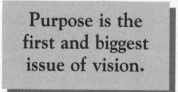

Purpose is the first and biggest issue of vision.

If you want to start a major argument in any church, ask the people, "What is our purpose here at (insert the name of your church)?" It may take the conversation a moment to get rolling, but after it starts it will be hard to stop. The answers will be varied, but will likely include preaching the gospel, evangelizing the lost, discipling the Christian, caring for the fellowship, providing for the widows and orphans, helping the hurting, educating the young, and even the keeping of the traditions of the church. Many of these will be stated in differing ways, but they will make the list in one form or another.

There are 485,000 identifiable churches in the United States today. I believe with all my heart that God has a specific purpose for every one of them.

The jigsaw puzzle of vision

Most of us have worked a jigsaw puzzle at some time or another. The most annoying ones have hundreds of pieces of which 90 percent are all the same color. Some of us love jigsaw puzzles, while many of us hate them (guess which camp I am in). Yet I have noticed that most of us share a common approach in how we start working the puzzle.

Where do you start working a jigsaw puzzle? Most people start with the border—the straight edge pieces. There are two reasons. The intelligent sounding reason is that when you get the border pieces in place you have a frame of reference for the entire puzzle. The real reason is that the border pieces are easier to work.

Vision is a lot like a jigsaw puzzle. You work it one piece at a time—and it takes a long time to get all the pieces in place. Discovering your purpose is the border of the puzzle. Your purpose will frame the rest of the vision. It needs to be easy to find, easy to see, easy to put together.   *our purpose statement*

> **Vision is a lot like a jigsaw puzzle. You work it one piece at a time— and it takes a long time to get all the pieces in place.**

This formula for frustration has been duplicated time and time again in churches around the world: try to determine your target or your strategy before you discover your purpose. In other words, try to determine programs and ministries without first discerning what it is

> **If you cannot state the purpose of your church in a single sentence statement, you have not yet discovered your purpose.**

that God wants you to do as a church. You will be frustrated in a big way—and will see very little fruit.

Many churches today have pulled together some kind of a purpose statement. It is a popular thing to do—and a useful thing to do as well. Use this principle for guidance. If you cannot state the purpose of your church in a single sentence statement, you have not yet discovered your purpose.

I once had a pastor hand me his purpose statement at a conference where I was speaking. It was a document that was three or four pages long. He asked me if I would evaluate it for him. I said, "I'd be glad to." I took one look at the purpose statement, handed it back to him, and said, "This won't work—it's too long." He replied, "But you didn't even take the time to read it." And I answered, "Bingo—and neither will your people."

Characteristics of a good purpose statement

These four characteristics of a good purpose statement can be used as a guideline. All four of these are vital.

- A good purpose statement is **biblical**. The Bible is our source for direction from God.

A hint: your purpose statement should fit within the parameters of the Great Commission. The five great commission statements that Jesus gave us (at the end of each of the gospels and at the beginning of Acts) were His marching orders for the church. Each of these are purpose statements in and of themselves.

> **Your purpose statement should fit within the parameters of the Great Commission.**

- A good purpose statement is **practical**. That means that it is written in simple, understandable, everyday terms. Your audience is your church—not a group of theologians.

- A good purpose statement is **transferable**. This simply means it can be passed easily and naturally from one person to the next.

- A good purpose statement is **short.** (This may be a concept that the other church leaders will have to explain to the preachers in the group.) Short means the goal is to be able to remember it, not to have to read it.

An acrostic worth using here for the four characteristics of a good purpose statement is KISSSS—which means keep it scriptural, simple, sharable, and short!

The first quest in defining vision is to discover your purpose.

2. Define your target

Discovering your purpose may be the most difficult part of defining vision. The most controversial and misunderstood part of vision is defining the target. The question in business jargon would be "Who is our primary customer?"

> **The most controversial and misunderstood part of vision is defining the target.**

The right questions

Curiosity is a virtue when it comes to determining our target. There are many questions that are asked in the process—some that are right and some that are wrong. The *right questions* that we must ask are:

- **Who is our immediate community?** That simply means who is right around your church. The reality is that church at its best is a local idea. This is why Jesus told us in Acts 1:8 that our first responsibility was to *"be witnesses in Jerusalem."* The question here is, "Who is our Jerusalem?"

  A church should reflect its community in makeup. Very few churches can become regional churches that draw from beyond their immediate community. The vast majority of churches are neighborhood churches—those churches that by definition reach the people in their neighborhood.

- **Who is our primary target?** I learned to shoot a bow and arrow while in the Cub Scouts. The first day, they lined us up and told us to shoot at the large bull's-eye targets that were twenty or so yards away. We shot every arrow we had in the general direction of those four or five targets. Few arrows found their mark. Before we began round number two, we were instructed to pick out a single target and shoot at the bull's-eye in the middle of that target. We were still a long ways from being excellent archers. But it was amazing how many more times we at least hit somewhere on the target when we focused on a single bull's-eye.

  Any church that is truly Christian wants to reach people

and will rejoice in any-
one that they reach. Any
person you reach for
Christ is somewhere on
your target. But we must
determine who is in the

> We must determine
> who is in the center
> of the bull's-eye on
> the target.

center of the bull's-eye on the target. Again the answer to
this question is most likely to be found by discovering who
is in your church's community.

- **Who has God put in this community that we are best
  equipped to reach?** Who you are as a church impacts who
  you can reach. You will tend to draw people like the ones
  you already have. At Flamingo Road Church, we won't
  reach very many non-English speaking Haitians even
  though there is a growing number in our area. (The main
  reason is that my Creole stinks. In fact, I have a hard
  enough time communicating in English.) Everyone wants
  to worship God in their native language. We have a grand
  mission church (a mission of one of our missions) that targets non-English speaking Haitians by offering worship in
  their native Creole.

The wrong questions

In an honest effort to define our target, we sometimes ask the
wrong questions. The *wrong questions* to ask are:

- **Who do we want to reach?** This question is wrong because
  it is too elitist. It ignores the fact that God "... *does not
  want any to perish, but everyone to come to repentance*" (2
  Peter 3:9).

- **Who are we already reaching?** This question is wrong

because it is too arrogant. It assumes you are already reaching the people you are supposed to reach.

Deer hunting churches

We don't do much deer hunting in South Florida, but I grew up in Texas and Oklahoma where deer hunting was a part of the norm. Ask any deer hunter this question and you will get the same answer: "If you want to hit your target dead center, what is the most important part of the rifle?"

The answer is the scope. Without the scope, any deer hunter can become really frustrated—because he won't get many deer—and he might make quite a mess.

Many churches are like well-intentioned but ineffectual deer hunters. They sit on the top of the hill overlooking their community with rifle in hand. They are shooting in every direction at everything that moves. They are killing cows. They are hitting rocks and trees. They are shooting up a storm and causing quite a commotion; but they aren't getting many deer.

This reminds me of a classic Peanuts cartoon. Charlie Brown is shooting arrows at his wooden fence. When the arrow hits the fence, he picks up his paint can and brush and paints a target around that arrow. When Lucy asks him what he is doing, he replies, "It's easier to hit the target this way."

Three realities of targeting

I believe there are *three realities of targeting* that are true in every church:

- When you aim at nothing, you hit nothing every time.

- When you aim at everything, you hit nothing most of the time.

- When you try to reach everyone, you reach no one most of the time.

No church reaches everyone

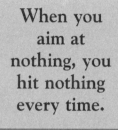

When you aim at nothing, you hit nothing every time.

As much as we would like to reach every person in our community, the reality is that no church reaches everyone. That is why a sovereign God has allowed 485,000 churches in America—to reach 485,000 different local communities of people. Each one reaches different people.

Flamingo Road Church is named after the road that it sits on (not after a soap opera). Along our stretch of Flamingo Road are four different church facilities in a row. There is a Methodist church that reaches conservative, middle-aged adults. There is a Pentecostal church that reaches mostly those with charismatic leanings. The Catholic church reaches traditional Catholics. Our church reaches unchurched young adults (many of whom are in fact former Catholics). Each of these churches reaches a different group of people within this same community.

Teammates—not competition

By the way—these churches are our teammates, not our competition. Fort Lauderdale is one of the most unchurched metropolitan areas in the country. According to our research, 90 percent of the people in our city do not attend any kind of church. If our goal were to reach those who are already in church, then churches might be our competition, because we would be targeting the 10 percent of the population that is already in church. But if our goal is to reach the unchurched, then other churches are our teammates.

Many church leaders today struggle with being territorial. I believe the reason for that is that our purpose and target is wrong. Jesus said it this way:

> *"I came to seek and to save that which was lost."*
>
> *Luke 19:10* (ASV)

> **We are to view other churches and other ministries as our teammates rather than our competition.**

In that one verse Jesus gives us his purpose—"to seek and to save"—and his target—"the lost." When Jesus was asked about other ministries, he replied *"Whoever is not against you is for you"* (Luke 9:50). That means we are to view other churches and other ministries as our teammates rather than our competition in reaching the community for Christ.

Whose territory?

Several years ago a new, young pastor moved to a church of about fifty people just up the road from us. He called me one day to ask a question. "Dan, I am doing a mailout. I plan to send it to the people in our church's zip code. I won't send it to the people in your church's zip code, but I wanted your permission to send it to the people in the zip code between us." I thanked him for his sweet, cooperative spirit. (May his tribe increase.) Then I said, "Rance, send it to anyone you like. Flamingo Road Church doesn't own any territory in the kingdom of God. We want your church to do well. We need all the help we can get in reaching the people of this community for Christ."

We are on record with the other churches in our area as being willing to help start a mission church across the street from us. In fact, fourteen of the sixteen missions and grand missions we have helped start are in this county. Most are within a fifteen to twenty minute drive of our location. Why? Because we are building *The* Kingdom, not *our* kingdom. The only way to reach a metropolitan area is by starting new churches—and lots of them!

It is interesting to me that some of the pastors of the largest churches in the country seem to struggle with this idea of territory. Several mega church pastors have said to me, "It is not possible to grow a big church and start missions at the same time." Of course it is possible—you just have to be secure enough to give up your tendency to be territorial. One local church pastor in

> **Arguing over who is going to reach the unchurched is like two ants arguing over who is going to eat the elephant.**

our area told one of our mission pastors, "We don't need any more churches in our county. Our church has it covered." What audacity! How can anyone say that a county with one and a half million people—90 percent of which are unchurched—does not need more churches because one large church has it covered?

Arguing over who is going to reach the unchurched is like two ants arguing over who is going to eat the elephant. No one is—unless we work together. George Barna tells us that on any given weekend, only about 37 percent of Americans are in church. That means there are plenty of unchurched people to go around. There is no room for being territorial in the kingdom of God.

The balance in targeting

> We are building *The* Kingdom, not *our* kingdom.

Here is the balance in targeting:

- We should welcome and celebrate anyone who walks in our doors.

- We should also define our primary target. We must know who is in the center of our bull's-eye.

For some of you this is a new idea. For others, this is an idea you have resisted.

Defining your target is biblical

Defining your target is a scriptural idea. Before some of you fall out of your easy chair, let me offer some specific examples:

- Paul's target was the Gentiles. *"I am the apostle to the Gentiles."* *(Romans 11:13)*

- Peter's target was the Jews. Paul confirmed this: *"I had been entrusted with the task of preaching the gospel to the Gentiles, just as Peter had been to the Jews."* *(Galatians 2:7)*

- James's target was the Jews who were being persecuted. He addressed his book *"to the twelve tribes scattered among the nations."* *(James 1:1)*

- Jeremiah's target was the king and the people of Judah. God sent Jeremiah to *"the kings of Judah, its officials, its priests and the people of the land."* (Jeremiah 1:18)

- Even Jonah had a reluctant target: the backslidden people of Nineveh. God told Jonah *"Go to the great city of Nineveh, and preach against it"* (Jonah 1:2). It is worth noting that God sent Jonah specifically to Nineveh and that Jonah passed several countries and people groups in route that also needed to repent. Why didn't he go to those groups? Because God had sent him to Nineveh.

Defining your target is a solid, biblical idea. How you define that target is major.

Define your target geographically

Rick Warren suggests four specific ways to define your target. First, you must define your target **geographically.** You won't reach many South Floridians in your ministry— unless your church is in South Florida.

> **Four specific ways to define your target:**
>
> - **geographically**
> - **demographically**
> - **culturally**
> - **spiritually**

While there are a few exceptions, your church's immediate target will be five to ten miles around your church. This number expands somewhat in rural settings. Your church's immediate target in driving time will be fifteen to twenty minutes. This area will expand slightly as you grow larger. Regional churches and mega churches draw from a larger area, but the majority of your people will come from close by. Church at its best is a local idea.

Define your target demographically

Second, you must define your target **demographically**. The easiest way to do this is to describe the community around you. You need to know as much as you can about who lives in your area. Demographic factors would include age, marital status, education level, occupation, and income. Ethnic background can also be important in areas with a large number of first generation immigrants. (Note: Nehemiah's target was the down-and-out Jews of Jerusalem.)

> You need to know as much as you can about who lives in your area.

Define your target culturally

The third way to define your target is **culturally**. I grew up in a variety of cultural settings. I spent the first few years of my life in the Oklahoma oil field. Those people were hard working rednecks. They drove pick-up trucks with gun racks across the cab and a bumper sticker that said, "You can have my gun when you pry my cold dead fingers off of it." My next childhood experience was in central Texas. People there were cowboys and ranchers. They wore their boots and their hats to church. The prominent feature in the church foyer was a hat rack. My next stop was North Dallas—which was yuppieville. White-collar executive types were the norm.

As a young adult I lived in Clinton, Mississippi. In that part of the country, it is still 1950. The manners and ways of the Old South prevail. I also lived in Southwest Florida. The people there are from the Midwest—from Michigan, Ohio, Indiana, and Illinois. Finally, I have settled in Southeast Florida. In Fort Lauderdale, people are generally from one of two places—New York or overseas. Hence our culture is dominated by Northerners and internationals.

Do you have to do church differently in each of those cultures? The answer is yes—if you want to be effective. The country music of central Texas will not fly in our part of Fort Lauderdale. The gentle ways of the Old South will not work in the oil field. You must do church differently for different cultures.

Today, many different cultures and subcultures can exist in the same community. This is especially true in urban settings. In Fort Lauderdale alone we have churches from many cultural backgrounds. Some of our churches are redneck; others are Old South in style and reach the people from Alabama and Georgia. Some are blue collar; others target the up and out. Some are truly international in mix; others are Island black or Hispanic or Haitian. Some are bilingual.

Which of these churches have the right target? All of them; because it takes multiple churches going after multiple cultures to reach all the people of a community.

> **You must do church differently for different cultures.**

Define your target spiritually

The fourth way we must define our target is **spiritually**. This is an area of targeting that few have intentionally thought through but that all churches in fact must do.

There are at least four spiritual target groups in every community:

- **The lost who are unchurched.** These are people who do not know Christ and do not attend any church.

- **The Christians who are unchurched**. These should more accurately be called dechurched people. They have been active in church at one point in their lives but are not currently attending. They have not quit on God but have quit on church.

- **New Christians**. These believers know Christ but are not mature. Church is still a new experience for them.

- **Mature Christians**. These believers have known Christ long term and are fully churched. (Hopefully they are also house-trained. Sorry about that—we have a new puppy.)

Most churches claim that their target is the lost. However, a closer examination of their strategy—their methods and programs—will tell you that their actual target is mature Christians. A non-Christian would not understand most of what they do because of the way they are doing it.

One way to know if you are hitting your target is the gifts that the pastors on staff receive. This can be both a humorous and a helpful form of evaluation. The first spontaneous gift I received after coming to Flamingo Road Church was a John McArthur commentary on Matthew. This was a gift from a new member who was a long-term, serious student of the Bible. He was typical of the people we were drawing at that time. One of my most recent gifts came from a seeker we had won to Christ. He was a totally unchurched man who had never been active in any kind of church. He is more typical of the person we draw now. He and his family had spent their Christmas holidays in Texas and brought me three uniquely

Texan gifts since he knew that I was a Texan. He came up to me after worship (with dozens of people standing in line to speak to me) and gave me the gifts. The first was a Big Red— which is a cherry flavored cream soda that is bottled in Waco, Texas. The second was a bottle labeled "Texas Sucker Puckering Hot Sauce." The third gift was the kicker—an ice cold Lone Star Beer. (In case you are wondering—I drank the Big Red, I shelved the hot sauce, and I kept the Lone Star Beer as a reminder of who we are after at Flamingo Road Church.)

First you must discover your purpose. Then you must define your target.

3. Decide your strategy

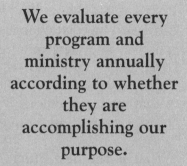

We evaluate every program and ministry annually according to whether they are accomplishing our purpose.

Churches often make two mistakes when it comes to strategy. The first mistake is that they define strategy before defining purpose and target. This is usually because they have a set of programs that they are already committed to and they intend to run those programs come hell or high water.

The second common mistake is that they are event driven rather than process driven in their strategy. The church calendar runs them rather than them running the church calendar. Once an event makes it onto the church calendar, it stays year after year without ever being evaluated in terms of accomplishing the purpose or reaching the target. (A quick side bar: at Flamingo Road, we evaluate every program and ministry annually according to whether they are accomplishing our purpose. Each one is reaffirmed, revised, or removed.)

If we are going to have a strategy that matches our purpose and target, there are several key questions that must be asked and answered:

- **What process will accomplish our purpose and reach our target?** Programs and events will not get the job done. There must be a deliberate process in place.

- **How do we move from where we are to where we want to go?** This is a big question—especially if you have major transitions to undertake.

- **What must change?** At Flamingo Road, one of our most obviously needed changes was in the area of defining our purpose and determining our target, which had never been done in our church.

- **What must not change?** You must determine what pieces of your strategy are nonnegotiable.

- **What is the best order of change?** For Flamingo Road, after we defined our purpose and determined our target, our music was one of our first strategy transitions.

You cannot find the right answers without asking the right questions—even when they are tough ones. So start asking!

> **You cannot find the right answers without asking the right questions.**

Wrap up

Defining vision is the most tedious and time consuming part of the vision process. But each church must take the time to discover its purpose, define its target, and determine its strategy—in that order.

Key Truth: The more specific the vision, the more dynamic the results.

Fuzzy vision leads to questionable results. Specific vision leads to dynamic results. If you want dynamic results, you must have specific vision.

You might want to take a minute to view our vision statement.

FLAMINGO ROAD CHURCH
FORT LAUDERDALE, FLORIDA
PURPOSE, TARGET & STRATEGY

PURPOSE: To honor God by leading people to become fully devoted followers of Jesus Christ.

TARGET: There are 750,000 people within a ten mile radius of our church. They are:

- 90 percent unchurched/dechurched—attend any church less than four times a year
- 80 percent uncommitted—never made a faith commitment to Jesus Christ
- 66 percent young adults and kids—ages birth to forty-five

Flamingo Frank is our composite target. He is thirty-four years old, unchurched, uncommitted to Christ, married with two kids, has a white-collar lifestyle, and is financially strapped.

STRATEGY: FULLY DEVOTED FOLLOWERS OF CHRIST

We use a twelve-step strategy organized around a baseball diamond:

1st base = commitment to membership

- I have committed my life to Christ
- I have completed the new members class

2nd base = commitment to maturity

- I am attending a weekly small group Bible study
- I am spending daily time with God
- I am giving my financial resources to God

3rd base = commitment to ministry

- I am serving in a ministry
- I am participating in ongoing training for ministry
- I am mentoring a leader

home plate = commitment to multiplication

- I am living an authentic Christian life
- I am building relationships with unchurched people
- I am sharing my faith story
- I am bringing my unchurched friends to church

Three quick comments about our purpose, target, and strategy statement:

- **It won't work in your setting** for two reasons. First, it does not fit your context. Your target will differ from ours;

therefore your strategy must differ as well. Second, it does not fit God's vision for your church. We serve a God who has a customized vision for every one of His churches.

- **We are continually revising our purpose, target, and strategy.** Our purpose has remained fairly constant over the past few years. Our target has changed in order to reflect new information as to who is in our community. Our strategy has changed greatly as we continually work to find new and improved ways to reach people for Christ.

- While you cannot copy any church's purpose, target, and strategy and use it as your own, you might be able to use our statement as a guide for writing your own vision. **Applications are not universally transferable; but principles are.**

Learning to fish

> We serve a God who has a customized vision for every one of His churches.

I learned to fish from my grandmother in rural Oklahoma. She had a tank behind her house (a hole in the ground that is not quite big enough to be called a pond). The necessary equipment was a shovel and a cane pole. We would use the shovel to dig up worms; then we would bait the hook and catch perch and catfish from her tank. That was fishing in Oklahoma.

I moved to Mississippi as a young adult and the time came to teach my three-year-old boy how to fish. We grabbed a shovel and a cane pole and headed for a nearby lake. When I stuck the shovel in the ground, the hole that I dug immediately filled up with water. As I was standing there contemplating what to do next, an old-timer walked by and asked, "What you doing?" I replied that I was trying to dig up some worms to use for bait. He informed me of three important facts: there were no worms in this part of the country, the fish in that lake were blue, gill, and the best bait for catching bluegill was bread. I thought to myself, "You can't catch fish with bread." But my son really wanted to fish. So we walked back to the house, got a piece of bread, and went for it. We caught thirty bluegill over the next thirty minutes. That was fishing in Mississippi.

> The hook is the gospel of Jesus Christ. It never changes ... the bait you put on the hook depends on where you are fishing and the kind of fish you are trying to catch.

I later moved to Southeast Florida. One day a friend invited me to go fishing with him in the famous Florida Everglades. I showed up at his house with my cane pole and some bread. He asked, "What's that for?" I replied, "I'm ready to go fishing." He informed me that the fish we were after were bass, that you need a rod and reel to catch them, and that the right bait for bass fishing was an artificial purple worm. I thought to myself, "You can't catch fish with an artificial worm." But we did. And that was fishing in Florida.

Which of these is fishing? All three. What is the constant in all three of my fishing experiences? The hook. The hook is the gospel of Jesus Christ. It never changes. If you are going to be a fisher of men, the gospel is central. But the bait you put on the hook depends on where you are fishing and the kind of fish you are trying to catch.

It sure is fun fishing when they are biting!

Step 3

Planting the Vision

After preparing for vision, you must define vision. After defining vision, you must plant the vision. You must plant the vision with the key leaders in your church, so that your vision can become their vision.

Vision is not a full grown fruit-producing tree. Vision is a seed, and like all seeds it must be planted in the proper soil in order to grow and bloom and bear fruit. If vision is a seed, then the proper soil is the hearts and minds of the leaders of your church.

A word of warning is needed at this point in the vision process. This step is the major fall down point for many churches. There

> Vision is a seed ...
> it must be planted
> in the proper soil.

are at least three reasons that the vision often dies before it gets planted in the hearts of the leaders of the church. First, our *tendency* to be excited about implementing the vision often causes us to move ahead without taking the time to get

67

other leaders on board. Second, the *theology* in many of our churches is so "top down" that many senior pastors don't think it is necessary to get other leaders on board. Third, our *track record* of having trouble getting leaders on board in the past tempts us to decide that it is easier to get forgiveness than permission. Fourth, many pastors and church leaders are too *threatened* to let go and let others own the vision.

> **Take the time to plant the vision with key leaders before sharing vision with the entire church.**

Just as we must take the time to prepare for vision before defining vision, we must now take the time to plant the vision with key leaders before sharing vision with the entire church. All you have at this point is the seed of vision. Where and how well you plant it are major issues.

In step three, I want to talk about planting the vision with a handful of key leaders. In step four, I will deal with including all the leaders as well as the remainder of the church.

Three sets of leaders are essential

1. Secure the approval of the power brokers

There are power brokers in every church. They are the E.F. Huttons that everyone listens to when they utter even a whisper. Every church has opinion makers. Some are people with formal influence due to a title or a position; others have informal influence due to personality or past experience or longevity. Every church has power brokers.

The power brokers in your church could include the chairman of the deacons or the elders. The head of the women's ministry is often a power broker. Mr. and Mrs. Charter Member can be power brokers followed close- ly by Mr. and Mrs. Been Here Forever. In some churches, Mr.

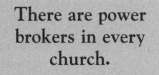

There are power brokers in every church.

and Mrs. Big Bucks are power brokers. Every church has power brokers. If you don't know who they are, wake up and smell the coffee.

Before you decide that this sounds more like secular politics than a scriptural principle, let me show it to you. Dealing with the power brokers in your circumstance is a biblical idea. That is exactly what Nehemiah had to do.

Nehemiah's power broker

For Nehemiah there was good news and bad news. The good news was he only had one power broker. The bad news was that the power broker was the king. The simple reality of his circumstance was this: to fulfill his vision, he had to secure the approval of the king. To fulfill the vision in your church, you will need to secure the approval of the power brokers as well.

A closer look at how Nehemiah did this gives some insight. Nehemiah secured the king's approval for several specific issues:

- **The overall plan.** Notice Nehemiah's initial request of the king:

  > *"If it pleases the king and your servant has found favor in his sight let him send me to the city in Judah where my fathers are buried so that I can rebuild it."*
  >
  > *Nehemiah 2:5*

Share your vision with the power brokers. Share from your heart. If you can't sell someone who has a vested interest, how will you sell someone with little or no interest? Any major change of plans requires the approval of the power brokers.

- **The timing of the plan.** Check out the next verse:

  Then the king, with the queen sitting beside him, asked me, "How long will your journey take, and when will you get back?" It pleased the king to send me, so I set a time.
  Nehemiah 2:6

Power brokers can be a big help in timing. They usually have a good sense of what is happening in the life of the church.

- **The details of the plan.** Nehemiah also shared the details concerning his journey.

  "letters to the governors ... provide me safe conduct ... a letter to the keeper of the king's forest ... timber to make beams ..."
  Nehemiah 2:7–8

- **The resources for the plan.** Nehemiah also shared about the resources he would need.

  The king had also sent army officers and cavalry with me.
  Nehemiah 2:9b

Power brokers often have needed resources at their disposal that they can make available.

If you secure the support of the power brokers, they will tend to back you as you implement the vision. If you fail to secure the support of the power brokers, they will tend to fight you. You have three basic choices with power brokers: get them on board, fight them, or run them off. Getting them on board is clearly the best and least hurtful choice.

> You have three basic choices with power brokers: get them on board, fight them, or run them off.

2. Secure the assistance of those whose help you will need

Once you have gained the approval of the power brokers, there are other key people who you will need to have on board. These leaders may not be the power brokers, but they are equally as important because of the help they can give you in making your transition.

For Nehemiah, there were two sets of people whose help he needed:

• The governors of the surrounding lands.

> *"If it pleases the king, may I have letters to the governors of Trans-Euphrates, so that they will provide me safe conduct until I arrive in Jerusalem."*
>
> Nehemiah 2:7

• The keeper of the forest.

> *"And may I have a letter to Asaph, the keeper of the king's forest, so he will give me timber to make beams."*
>
> Nehemiah 2:8

Whose help will you need?

For the church, there are also two sets of people whose help you need to secure before beginning any transition.

• Secure the assistance of *the leaders whose territory you are going through.*

  Nehemiah went through several municipalities on his way to Jerusalem. He therefore needed to get permission for safe passage through these lands.

  In the days of the old West, trespassers were often killed for coming through someone's territory without permission. If you don't get permission before you go through someone's territory in the church, you might get your scalp handed to you as well.

  For example, if you are going to transition the music in the church, you better get the worship leadership on board on the front end. If you want to change the role of the deacons, you will need the assistance of the chairman. If you are going to change the women's ministry, you will need a miracle as well as the help of the leader of that ministry.

  We really blew this idea in a big way more than once during our transitions. When we began transitioning our music, we decided to replace the organ with a band. So we had the organ removed. The problem was we left out one important detail: we forgot to tell the organist. She came on Sunday morning ready to play. This was not our best moment. By the grace of God and because of her maturity, this lady is still with us today. But we caused her some hurt that was unnecessary.

It may be easier to get forgiveness than permission; but when it comes to transitions, it is rarely the wisest choice. Secure the assistance of the leaders whose territory you are going through.

> **It may be easier to get forgiveness than permission; but when it comes to transitions, it is rarely the wisest choice.**

- Secure the assistance of *the providers of the resources you are going to need*.

Nehemiah needed timber to build. Without it his project was going nowhere. Rather than just plunge ahead and figure that God will provide (like some people I know who are sometimes more spiritual than the Bible), Nehemiah secured the assistance of the keeper of the forest before he started his journey.

Key resource people need to be secured whenever possible before you begin your transitions. This would include those who are going to be asked to give their time, their talents, and their ideas as well as those who may be asked to give of their financial resources.

If you go it alone

Some of you may be thinking that taking the time to get these people on board is unnecessary. If you do not take the time to secure the assistance of the key leaders you will cause four things to happen.

- **You will cause confusion for the church.** When a

recognized leader does not know what is going on, the result is confusion in the church. The parallel would be a captain who does not know what the general has planned until the orders come down the line. The result is confusion among the rank and file.

- **You will cause people to entrench.** When people are not included in the change process, they can feel that you are taking their church away from them. This causes them to feel threatened. They often react by digging in and waiting for you to change or leave.

- **You will cause leaders to leave the church.** A leader that is uninformed often feels unwanted and unneeded. Most leaders have a high need to be informed, wanted, and needed. If you will not keep them in the loop, they will find a church that will.

- **You will cause great hurt for yourself.** Hurt because of the confusion. Hurt for the leaders that are leaving. Hurt from the doubt that is cast on your vision. You may be tough enough to handle the hurt, but wounded leaders do not make good decisions.

If these four results of not getting your leaders on board sound personal, that is because we have experienced them first hand here at Flamingo Road. This was our most glaring mistake in the vision process. We simply did not do a good job of getting all of the leaders on board before we began to make our transitions. The good news is that God honored His vision and blessed our transitions even though we blew this step. The bad news is we caused ourselves and the church some unnecessary hurt and confusion and lost some leaders we did not have to lose. This was one of our toughest moments in the

transition process—and we brought it on ourselves.
Take the time to secure the help that you are going to need
along the way.

3. Seek the advice of your vision team

Securing the approval of the power brokers is pretty much a
no-brainer. Securing the assistance on the front end of those
whose help you will need on the journey is also a common
sense issue. This third group of key leaders—the vision team
—is often overlooked in our churches.

The most effective leaders know the value of a vision team.
Every visionary needs a small handful of leaders who can help
dream the dream. One reason that many of us discover that it
is, in fact, lonely at the top is that we have not surrounded
ourselves with a vision team to help us accomplish the task.
We are often alone because we have chosen to be alone.

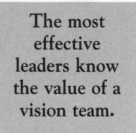

The most effective leaders know the value of a vision team.

Consider the effective leaders in the
Bible who had a handful of close
confidants:

- King David led an army of thousands, including hundreds of
  select troops, with thirty leaders
  and three mighty men.

- Nehemiah used hundreds to rebuild the wall, scores of
  leaders, and a handful of choice men for his vision team.

- Jesus taught tens of thousands, fed the multitude, sent out
  seventy, spent time discipling twelve, and had three in his
  inner circle.

> You need the vision team for feedback, for balance, for accountability, and for fellowship.

Effective visionaries have a small group of their sharpest leaders as a vision team. This vision team is especially important for any leader who is leading a church through major transition. You need them for feedback, for balance, for accountability, and for fellowship. Whatever you do— don't depart on your vision journey without them!

Principles for working with your vision team

There are several principles that we can gain from seeing how Nehemiah worked with his vision team.

First, choose your vision team carefully. We do not know how Nehemiah chose his vision team. The Bible does not tell us. We can assume from his attention to detail and the successful completion of his vision that he chose them very carefully and very well.

Common sense would suggest the following criteria for choosing your vision team:

- **Choose mature believers.** Leadership is formative. The church never rises above the level of its leadership. Any one who understands this idea should see the need for mature believers on the vision team. It is tempting to put some younger, newer Christians on the team for the sake of their younger, newer ideas. If they do not possess the necessary maturity, it is not worth the trouble they can cause. The depth of the vision team may well determine the depth of the vision. Immature believers on a vision team will cause you to have an incomplete vision.

- **Choose dreamers rather than detail people.** Most people in the world fit neatly into one of these groups. They are either a dreamer—which means that they love to think big, reach high, tend to be optimistic-and see the sky as the limit. Or they are a detailer—which means they love to figure out the details, relish policies and procedures, tend to be realists, and see resources as limitations.

There is a time and a place for detail people. There is a real need in the church for those who love to ask what will it cost, how will we do that, who is going to be responsible, and who will pay for it. There is a time and place for those who love policies and procedures and detailed plans —but the vision team is not it.

The members of your vision team need to be big picture people. They need to be dreamers and visionaries whose favorite question is "What if?" To dream the dream, you need dreamers. To carry out the dream, you need detailers. At this point, you are still dreaming the dream. You need dreamers who realize the need for the vision to be big enough that people will say "I will give my life to this."

> The members of your vision team need to be big picture people.

- **Choose trustworthy people.** Let me be plainer than that: you need people on your vision team who can keep their mouths shut. Nothing shoots vision in the foot quicker than it being leaked before it is fully formed or before the time is right for it to be shared with the entire church.

Choosing the right vision team is major. I would offer two other practical suggestions for choosing your vision team.

- **Consider staff first.** I would suggest that your church staff be the first group you consider for the vision team. At Flamingo Road, the pastors on the staff have been our vision team for several years. This group was originally three pastors; it now numbers seven.

  I am often asked at this point, "What if the staff cannot dream?" My response is usually threefold. First, you may have the wrong people on staff. Second, you may need to add staff that can dream. Third, you may need to bypass certain staff members and choose dreamers from within the congregation.

  If you are the only staff member in your church, you will need to find laymen who can be volunteer staff and serve on your vision team as well. Don't make the mistake of trying to go it alone.

- **Keep the vision team small.** In my experience, a team of three to seven is a great size. If the vision team gets bigger than that, it is really difficult to dream and plan.

Second, work quietly behind the scenes. After you choose your vision team, you must put them to work behind the scenes. Nehemiah led his vision team to do its work out of the public view.

> *I set out during the night with a few men. I had not told anyone what my God had put in my heart to do for Jerusalem.*
> *Nehemiah 2:12a*

The officials did not know where I had gone or what I was doing, because as yet I had said nothing to the Jews or the priests or nobles or officials or any others who would be doing the work. Nehemiah 2:16

> **The point of working behind the scenes is not to be secretive; the point is to be strategic.**

Not only is working quietly behind the scenes smart—it is scriptural. The point of working behind the scenes is not to be secretive; the point is to be strategic. There is a right time and place for everyone in the church to be involved in the vision, but that time is not as it is being formed. Dreaming it must be done with a small group.

Third, survey the current conditions. Here is how Nehemiah and his vision team did this.

By night I went out ... examining the walls of Jerusalem, which had been broken down, and its gates, which had been destroyed by fire. Nehemiah 2:13

You must take an honest and objective look at your current conditions. This includes an objective assessment of what is broken down and not working in the church. So make a list based on your purpose and your target. The list should include what is working in one column and what is not working in the other. Stop for a moment now and jot down whatever comes to your mind. What is working in your church? There should be several things that come to mind. Now make a quick list of what is not working. If you can come up with those in just a few seconds, what could you come up with if you worked at it?

Fourth, share your vision and your heart with your vision team. Nehemiah did this really well:

> *"You see the trouble we are in: Jerusalem lies in ruins, the gates have been burned with fire. Come, let us rebuild the wall of Jerusalem, and we will no longer be in disgrace."*
>
> *Nehemiah 2:17*

Sharing your vision with the vision team is vital—and sharing your heart with them is equally important. Tell them your dream. Share with them your heartache as

> **Sharing your vision with the vision team is vital— and sharing your heart with them is equally important.**

well. They need to know how you got to this point—so tell them what God is doing in your heart and in your life.

> *I also told them about the gracious hand of my God upon me and what the king had said to me."*
>
> *Nehemiah 2:18a*

Check out the response of Nehemiah's vision team when he shared his vision and his heart:

> *They replied, "Let us start rebuilding." So they began this good work.*
>
> *Nehemiah 2:18b*

Sharing your heart with your vision team is major. A large part of our success at Flamingo Road is due to the fact that we keep our vision team (the pastors on our staff) on the same page. We meet every week for staff meeting. We eat out together for lunch at least twice every week. We spend time in each other's homes hanging out. When we are out of town, we stay in touch via the phone or e-mail. We spend enough time together to work as a team. A long time church member told me recently, "You guys fit together so well that you can finish each other's sentences." That is because we work hard at staying on the same page.

We also work hard at keeping the entire leadership team up to speed. The most important time in our church schedule is a once-a-month leadership team meeting. One Sunday night each month all the leaders of Flamingo Road Church get together for a time of training and vision casting. This time is so vital that the pastors on the staff have made the decision that we do not miss leadership team meeting. We arrange our time away from the church to make sure we are in town for leadership team night. We want our leaders to know how important and valuable they are to us. We also require all leaders in the church to be a regular part of leadership team. If you are not willing to train and be a part of the team, you cannot lead at Flamingo Road Church.

Wrap up

In order to plant the vision with the key leaders in the churches you must give attention to three groups of leaders. You must secure the approval of the power brokers. You must secure the assistance of those whose help you are going to need. You must seek the advice of your vision team. Getting these three groups of leaders on board can determine whether the vision succeeds.

Key Truth: Expose your key leaders to model churches.

Your key leaders need to be exposed to model churches. (Aren't you glad I didn't just say "expose your key leaders?")

It is nothing short of sheer genius to figure out a way to expose your leaders to a model church. If a picture is worth a thousand words, then a living model is worth a million.

Go to school on churches that are purpose driven. Identify some parallel ministries that are similar to your own. It will be really helpful to find some churches that are in the

> **If a picture is worth a thousand words, then a living model is worth a million.**

process of making the same transitions you are about to undertake. They will have insights and ideas that will prove to be helpful to you as you make your transitions.

Those of you who have trouble with studying model churches might want to know that you have a problem with Scripture. Learning from model churches is clearly a biblical idea. Look at what Paul wrote about learning from model churches:

> *You became imitators of us and of the Lord ... and so you became a model to all the believers in Macedonia and Achaia ... your faith in God became known everywhere.*
> *1 Thessalonians 1:6–8*

Paul was a model for the Thessalonians; then they became a model for other churches.

Note: Several of the "key transition truths" throughout this book are adapted from Rick Warren's lesson entitled *Leading Your Church Through Change* which is a part of Saddleback's Purpose Driven Church Conference.

Learn two ways

There are two ways to learn in life: from personal experience and from the experience of others. The first way is to insist on learning it all yourself and spend many years in the school of hard knocks. The other way is to go to school on the experience of others and save yourself and your church many heartaches. The best and brightest of leaders are experts in both types of learning.

> **There are two ways to learn in life: from personal experience and from the experience of others.**

You cannot transfer specific applications from one church setting to another. But you can transfer principles. Several churches have served as models for us here at Flamingo Road, but we are not copies of any of them. In church we must learn two ways: from personal experience you learn what God wants to do in your church, and from others you can learn some creative ways to get there.

Why do we need to learn both by personal experience and from the experience of others? First—you do not have enough time to learn everything by personal experience. Second— the stakes are too high. People are dying all around us without Christ. Let's get to it!

Step 1: Preparing for vision
Step 2: Defining the vision
Step 3: Planting the vision

Step 4

Sharing the Vision

Take a moment to review where you are in the vision process. You have taken the time to prepare for vision by collecting information about your community, becoming discontent with the status quo, fasting, praying, and waiting on God. You have defined your vision in terms of your purpose, your target, and your strategy. You have planted the vision in the minds and hearts of your key leaders and have brought your vision team fully on board.

If you have given adequate attention to preparing, defining, and planting the vision, by this time you are ready to share the vision with the whole church. In fact, you are about to explode with the vision that has filled your heart. You are at an "If I don't share this vision soon I am going to burst" place. That is a good place to be!

Let's reconnect with Nehemiah. Like you, he has only shared his vision with a few leaders.

The officials did not know where I had gone or what I was doing, because as yet I had said nothing to the Jews or the priests or nobles or officials or any others who would be doing the work.   Nehemiah 2:16

So far only three groups of leaders within the church know of your vision: the power brokers, those whose help you will need, and the vision team. Now it is time to share the vision with two other groups of people.

1. Share your vision with the remaining leaders

Now is the time to get the entire leadership team of the church on board. Not just the power brokers, resource providers, and visionaries you have already included; all the leaders must be challenged with the vision. This would include every teacher, worker, helper, and assistant. Any one with any responsibility in the life of the church must be included.

Leaders first, church second

Before vision is shared with the church from the pulpit, it must be shared with the entire leadership team. Nothing devalues and alienates a leader as quickly as not knowing what is coming next before the rank and file know.

> **Nothing devalues and alienates a leader as quickly as not knowing what is coming next before the rank and file know.**

Imagine that you have been a lay leader in your church for a long time. You trust your church staff but also like to know what is going on. You are sitting in church one morning when the pastor announces a new vision plan for the church. When the service has concluded, several of your friends—who know you are a leader in the church—ask you what you think about the new plan. The only reply you can make is, "I didn't know anything about it."

> **It is very difficult for leaders who do not know what is going on to support it.**

Sounds ridiculous, right? It is ridiculous—and it happens all the time in many churches. It is very difficult for leaders who do not know what is going on to support it wholeheartedly. Most leaders have a built-in need to know.

You have to read between the lines a bit to see that Nehemiah was careful to include all his leaders in the vision. In Nehemiah 2:16 he tells us clearly that *"the priests or nobles or officials or any others who would be doing the work"* did not yet know of the vision. The next chapter lists all the priests and officials and other leaders who are heading up the work on different portions of the wall. What happened in between? Nehemiah shared his vision with the remaining leaders and got them to buy into it.

Let me say this again: it is a major mistake to not take the time to share your vision with all of your leadership team before sharing it with the rest of the church. Leaders who hear about changes in direction and focus from the pulpit are not likely to support those changes.

Leaders typically fall into one of two categories when a new vision plan is formulated. If your leaders are on board before you share the vision with the whole church, they will usually be your allies. They will help those who struggle with the changes to get on board. If your leaders are not on board before you share the vision with the whole church, they will usually be your enemies and will lead others to resist the changes.

Here's a practical suggestion: take all of your leadership away on a vision retreat. A simple Friday night and Saturday get-away will suffice. Use the time away to take them through the vision process and bring them up to speed. Advantages include building unity, giving time for questions to be asked and answered, and letting your leadership team become owners and carriers of the vision.

We have a Presbyterian church here in town that was facing a challenge. They were a church of 200 in worship attendance in a downtown area. They were not growing and they were not reaching the young adults who were moving into their area. Their leaders decided to start a second worship service and to make it contemporary in style. Before making this change, they took fifty leaders on a leadership retreat. I had the privilege of meeting with this group shortly thereafter. They were fired up and ready to go! They have since started their service—and it is working.

Whatever you have to do, get the remainder of your leadership team on board before you share your vision with the remainder of the church.

2. Share your vision with the remainder of the church

Now it is time to share the vision with the entire church. It is time for all the people—whose buy in is crucial—to be included. When it is all said and done, it is the people of the church that will complete the vision.

The success of any vision comes down to one issue: will the majority of the people of the church get behind it? Joshua without his people would have been a conqueror without an invasion force. David without his people would have been just another

> The success of any vision comes down to one issue: will the majority of the people of the church get behind it?

king without an army. Nehemiah without the people of Jerusalem would have been a project manager without workers. Every leader must be able to sell his vision to his followers.

The easiest way to tell if you are a leader is to look behind you and see if you have any followers. There is a Chinese proverb that says, *"He who thinks he leads but has no followers is only taking a walk."* Now is the time to find out if you are leading or just out for a walk.

As you read chapter three of Nehemiah, you come to an astonishing realization: the majority of the people are working on the wall. The people caught the vision! God gave the vision to Nehemiah, Nehemiah shared it with his leaders, and together Nehemiah and his leaders gave it to the people. The baton of vision was successfully passed from the visionary to the leaders to the people.

Key Truth: Since vision is both caught and taught, it must be shared in multiple ways.

We work continually to present vision in multiple ways at Flamingo Road. The reason is simple: people catch vision in different ways. To get your vision to as many people as possible, you must share it in as many ways as possible.

Ten ways to share vision

All ten of these methods for sharing vision have been effective for us at Flamingo Road. I recommend them to you.

- **Preaching.** Never underestimate the power of the pulpit when it comes to vision. I suggest that a study of the book of Acts can be an especially powerful tool for sharing vision. In the nine years I have been on the staff at Flamingo Road Church, there is only one passage of scripture I have preached through three times: the first half of the book of Acts. All three times I kept asking the question "What is a New Testament church like?" One series went like this:

  How does a New Testament church pray? (Acts 1)
  How does a New Testament church fellowship? (Acts 2)
  How does a New Testament church worship? (Acts 2)
  How does a New Testament church give? (Acts 4)
  What do deacons do in a New Testament church? (Acts 6)
  How does a New Testament church do missions? (Acts 11)
  How does a New Testament church choose missionaries? (Acts 13)
  How does a New Testament church make decisions? (Acts 15)

Some piece of vision should be shared in every sermon that is preached. We now organize our preaching and teaching at Flamingo Road around our twelve-step strategy. There are four of the pastors on staff who share the teaching in our worship services. Regardless of who is speaking, one of those twelve steps is highlighted in every sermon. This keeps our vision constantly in front of our people. We also do a vision series once a year in order to revisit our purpose, target, and strategy.

- **Small group vision studies.** Last fall, one of our pastors wrote an adult small group curriculum based on our purpose and twelve-step strategy. Every adult class in the church went through this vision study.

- **Purpose statements.** Once you have condensed your purpose into a single sentence statement (as discussed in step two), you can use it to communicate vision. We find ways to refer to and repeat our purpose statement regularly. Anyone who has been at Flamingo Road for more than a few months can tell that our purpose is *"to honor God by leading people to become fully devoted followers of Christ."*

- **Vision phrases.** Don't forget the power of a phrase—or a slogan—to communicate vision. Short, catchy phrases can be used to communicate small pieces of vision. Several of these have worked their way into the life of our church. Phrases like *"play to an audience of one"* and *"church for the unchurched"* have become part of who we are. Our most repeated phrase has become our motto: *"whatever it takes."*

- **Vision verses.** Every visionary church needs a handful of life verses that become the heart and soul of the church. Whenever I think of Rick Warren and Saddleback church, the great commission and the great commandment are the verses that come to my mind. I have heard Willow Creek pastor Bill Hybels teach from Luke 15 (the "lost" parables) and from Acts 2 (a Biblically functioning community) on several occasions. Two passages that really matter to us at Flamingo Road are Luke 19:10 (*"I came* *to seek and to save that which was lost")* and 1 Corinthians 2:9 *("No eye has seen, no ear has heard, no mind has conceived what God has prepared for those who love him.")*

- **Faith stories.** We first called these testimonies. Then we realized that testimony is a word that is used only in courtrooms and in churches. Seekers do not understand that terminology, so we now call them faith stories. We have a faith story in most of our weekend worship services. We invite someone from the church to share their story of faith in Christ. These faith stories are usually given mid-sermon. They serve as great illustrations of points in the lesson. (It also serves as a great alarm clock for those who have dosed off during the sermon.)

In order to coordinate these stories with the sermon, we have asked our leaders to write out their faith stories. We then take them, categorize them by subject (i.e., grief, job loss, loneliness, faith) and file them. When we have a lesson coming up on a related topic, we turn to that file. These faith stories are always written out and read. This helps the giver of the story to stay on time and gives them a needed script if they get emotional.

This past weekend we had a powerful faith story. The lesson was on How to Make Changes That Last. One of the major points in the teaching dealt with how God uses the difficult circumstances of our lives as change agents. Earlier that week, Hurricane George had come close enough to South Florida to cause all of us to improve our praying. Years earlier, Hurricane Andrew had leveled the house of one of our families—while they were still in it! When I got to the part of the lesson that focused on circumstances, I asked Grecy, the lady of the house, to share her faith story of how God spared their lives and used that difficult circumstance to blow their family into fuller service for him. It was a great moment that grabbed everyone's attention.

> **Faith stories are "God at work" moments.**

We still occasionally do drama in our weekend services, but I would much rather have a faith story. It is the power of a living example instead of a reenacted example. Faith stories are "God at work" moments. Those who hear us preach will forget our sermons. They won't forget those faith stories.

- **Conferences.** Another way to catch vision is through conferences. Leith Anderson once told me there are 30,000 pastors conferences in America each year. I believe in going to them. But I only go to the ones that teach truths that fit what is happening at Flamingo Road. If you are looking for a conference on leadership, I encourage you to attend one of Willow Creek's events. If you are trying to grasp how to organize your church around vision and purpose, Saddleback's conference on *The Purpose Driven Church* is the best I have found. If you are in a traditional church that is trying to transition, you may want to attend one of our conferences at Flamingo Road on *Leading Your Church Through Transition*. There are some excellent conferences out there. Be purpose driven; choose which ones to attend based on your need.

- **Tapes and books.** You may not be able to take all of your church leaders to the conference of your choice, but you can bring the material to them in the form of tapes and books. Rick Warren's *The Purpose Driven Church* is required reading for our leaders. Leith Anderson's classics *Dying for Change* and *Church for the Twenty-first Century* are must reading as well. James Emery White has written a great book called *ReThinking the Church*. Doug Murren's books *Baby Boomerang* and *Leadershift* are challenging and will stretch your thinking. *Inside the Mind of Unchurched Harry and Mary* by Lee Strobel is a big help in understanding seekers. Tapes are a great resource as well; they are less expensive and can be listened to while driving to work.

- **One on one**. This may be the most overlooked method of sharing vision. Let me illustrate it this way: how do you catch a cold? My mother used to tell me that you catch a cold when you go outside in cold weather without enough clothes to keep you warm. Mom did not miss many things—but she missed this one. How do you catch a cold? You must be exposed to someone who has a cold. You must hang out with someone who is sick. How do you catch vision? You must be exposed to someone who has vision. You must hang out with visionaries.

> How do you catch vision? You must be exposed to someone who has vision. You must hang out with visionaries.

You may have some old guard leaders in your church who cannot catch the vision from the pulpit. But if you take them to lunch and say, "John, my heart is really burdened for these young adults in our community. We are not reaching them at church, and I think God wants us to reach them. What do you think we should do?" What will John's reaction be? First, he is going to be relieved because he thought he was in trouble when you called him and made a lunch appointment. Second, he is going to be honored that you are asking his opinion. So you listen to John and share your heart with him one on one. Two weeks later when you see John at church, you just might hear him saying to his friends, "You know, pastor Dan and I went to lunch the other day. We think we need to make some changes around here to reach the young adults in our community. What do you think?"

- **Living it out in your own life.** You cannot expect a church to catch a vision that you are not living out in your own life. They won't catch it if you are not living it. They will never be any more committed to reaching seekers than you are. When you are living it and can talk about it from firsthand experience, it will catch on.

> You cannot expect a church to catch a vision that you are not living out in your own life.

I play softball on Friday nights in a secular league. There are two reasons I do not play in a church league. First, the worst behavior I have ever seen in my life is in church softball leagues. Second, I want to be with seekers—with lost people—with pagans.

I do not show up at the softball game with a sign on my chest that says "Dan Southerland, one of the pastors at Flamingo Road Church." I keep that a secret. I am just a guy who wants them to know that I am a Christian.

Let me give a specific example. Our church produces a Christmas pageant every year. It is designed to be a first touch event for our people to bring their unchurched friends. The pageant ends with four of our pastors singing together—including me. We now rent a musical theater that seats thousands to hold this pageant. But years ago we held the pageant in the local high school where we were also holding our Sunday worship services.

One night I met a new player on the softball field before we started the game. She said "I know you from somewhere—but I can't figure it out." I went out to second base as the game started and she sat on the bench. Halfway through the game, in the middle of an inning, she yelled out "I know who you are. You are one of those guys who sings in that Christmas show at the high school. Do you go to that church?" At this point the game stopped as everyone turned and looked at me. I later shared with my new friend that I did go to that church and I invited her to attend. She did so—and was a bit shocked when she saw me in the pulpit preaching.

I play lousy second base, and I only hit a little bit better than I field. But I love hanging out with unchurched people. I love the challenge of deliberately building relationships with unchurched people. Today there are eight different families that have come to be a part of Flamingo Road church through Friday night softball and through the other community teams I coach. That is what I call purpose driven playing.

If you want your folks to catch the vision, you better live it out—on and off the playing field. You must model vision. You must be able to say "I do this!"

Wrap up

You cannot fake passion. As you share your vision with the remaining leaders and with the entire church, share your heart. If you want them to be passionate about the vision, you must be passionate about it. If you want them to live it out, you must live it out. Share your vision with your people. Keep sharing it until they catch it.

Step 1: Preparing for vision
Step 2: Defining the vision
Step 3: Planting the vision
Step 4: Sharing the vision

Step 5

Implementing the Vision

This fall my son started high school. He has looked forward to this moment for years—not because he loves school or gets into the social scene. Starting high school means one thing to Jered: a chance to play football. In South Florida, none of the public schools offer football at the elementary or middle school level. So for years he has played every other sport there is, just to bide his time and wait for football.

He made the junior varsity squad as a freshman and was looking forward to his first game. The coach informed him that he would be playing both ways—starting at halfback on offense and at defensive end. He was so pumped. The day of the big game came with great anticipation but ended with disappointment. It was rained out. He worked his way through the let down and looked forward to the next game. Game number two was canceled due to a hurricane warning. Again he put his mind toward the next game. Game three was scheduled for a Monday afternoon and the forecast called for perfect weather. He arrived at school with flowers in his hand for his favorite cheerleader—only to learn that the game had again been postponed.

Even as I write this, Jered is still waiting for a chance to get on the field. He has been practicing since August tenth is first game will be October third. My prediction is that he will be so wired up by the time that he gets to play that he will destroy the first running back that comes his way. (A quick update: Jered ran for a twenty-one yard gain his first play from scrimmage.)

Ready to roll

If you have been working through the steps of preparing, defining, planting, and sharing your vision, by now you are worked up and ready to get into the game. You are ready to implement some changes. Before you charge ahead, please take note of the fact that you are just now halfway through this eight-step vision process. Even though you are halfway through, you are just now implementing changes.

> **Most churches spend far too little time in preparation and move far too quickly into making changes.**

Most churches spend far too little time in preparation and move far too quickly into making changes. You could say they rush in where angels fear to tread. There is a reason that many churches that try to make major transitions fail: they don't take the time to work through the vision process. If you are in a hurry, please don't lead your church to change. All that will change is the current address on your resume.

Principles to apply in implementing vision

1. Implement your changes one at a time

This past spring we did a teaching series called "Celebrate Recovery." It is a series we based on Rick Warren's *Road to Recovery* series. The fifth lesson in that series is called *Making Changes*. My greatest concern in that lesson was that people would get so fired up that they would identify a dozen different changes they needed to make and would try to make them all at once.

You can't do that. If you try to change a dozen things in your life at one time, you just get frustrated. If you try to change a dozen things in your church at one time, you will get frustrated—but you won't be alone. Everyone in the church will be as frustrated as you are.

> **What works when it comes to change? Focusing on one change at a time.**

What works when it comes to change? Focusing on one change at a time. In your personal life, you must focus on one character flaw at a time. In the life of the church, you must focus on one vision change at a time. The old saying is true: change by the yard is hard; change by the inch is a cinch.

One of my concerns at our conference on transitions is that the church leaders who come will go home with a list of a dozen changes they want to make. That is not a problem. But if they try to implement all those changes at once—that is a problem.

Nehemiah started with a single project. He decided to begin with the gates. His first work crews appear in chapter three and they are all organized around the gates of the city (see Nehemiah 3:1,3,6,13,14,15,28).

2. Implement your changes in a strategic order

As a child, one of the highlights of summer was eating ice cold watermelon. Mom would cut open a big melon and turn us loose in the backyard. For a few moments we would be content to munch on melon. But inevitably the event would deteriorate into a watermelon seed fight.

The best part of trying to squirt a watermelon seed is that you never know for certain where it is going to go. I would be trying to shoot a seed at one of my brothers across the table and I would hit my best friend—who was sitting beside me. Or I would have my sister in my sights and would put just a bit too much pressure and the seed would go straight up and come down and hit me on the head. You could never quite tell what was going to happen in a watermelon seed fight—but it was going to be sloppy.

Often church leaders suffer from watermelon seed-style leadership. Rather than have an order in their work, they run from project to project—over here one minute, over there the next, then back over here, then somewhere else. You can never tell where they are headed because they rarely hold a straight course for any extended period of time. The worst part of watermelon seed leadership is that it confuses the hooey out of your followers. About the time they get lined up and think they know where you are headed, you spurt off in a new direction. Soon they quit following and just watch you run in circles (which is a lot less tiring and a lot more entertaining for them).

What order?

As you work through the process of vision, you will identify many changes that need to be made. You must put them in a strategic order. Nehemiah did this. If you study the work pattern in chapters three and four, you will discover a strategic order in his project. He tackled the gates first, the walls second, and the finishing touches last.

No one but God can give you the strategic order for your transitions.

One of the questions I am asked most often is "What is the right order for implementing changes?" Some may not like the two answers that I give. First, no one but God can give you the strategic order for your transitions. He promises wisdom when we seek him:

> *If any of you lacks wisdom, he should ask God, who gives generously to all without finding fault, and it will be given to him.*
> James 1:5

If you have found God's vision, God will also show you the right order to implement the changes that are needed.

Second, the order of change is different in every church. If God has a unique purpose and plan for each church, then the path to that purpose will also be unique.

While I cannot tell you the order of change for your church, I can offer you this suggestion. The right plan for change will probably follow the purpose, target, and strategy order. Changes in purpose

The order of change is different in every church.

> **The right plan for change will probably follow the purpose, target, and strategy order.**

should be made first. Changes in target should be made next. Changes in strategy—which are the most visible changes—should be made last.

At Flamingo Road, we had to make the transitions in our purpose and our target before we could make any major transitions in worship style. To transition our worship style from traditional to contemporary just because we like it better that way is not an improvement. No one style of worship is better than any other. In our setting, it simply made sense to change to a contemporary style of worship after we had decided that our main target was unchurched young adults.

List the changes you need to make. Put them in a strategic order. Then tackle them one at a time.

3. Put key leaders to work in visible places

Nehemiah knew the principle of leader visibility. He knew that he needed to place his best and most well-known leaders in visible places of leadership. So he put his best leaders to work first on the gates (again see Nehemiah 3:1,3,6,13,14,15, 28).

Why put them on the gates? Because in a city with half-torn-down walls, all the people would come and go through the gates. You could not come and go from the city without seeing the leaders at work. And when the people saw the leaders working, they were willing to work as well.

As we began making transitions at Flamingo Road, some of our more traditional leaders left us. At the same time, we began drawing fewer traditional Christians and more seekers. That meant that we really had to capitalize on putting the leaders we did have in visible places. One example of leader visibility occurred on Saturday nights. When we first began our Saturday night service, we wanted to start small groups on Saturday night as well. The plan was a 6:00 worship time followed by age-graded small groups at 7:15. In order to insure that the Saturday night small groups would make it, we went to some of our strongest Sunday morning classes and challenged our best teachers to move to Saturday night—and to bring their class with them. We asked them to be missionaries for a year. We hoped that they would draw additional people to Saturday night—and they did!

A second example of leader visibility came when we were beginning to transition our Sunday morning services to a contemporary style. The Saturday night contemporary service was working so well that we decided to transition our Sunday morning services to the same style. To do so we asked our leaders for a specific commitment. We also asked them to sit down front during the worship services and be participatory so the rest of the church could see that they were supportive. Some of those early leaders could not clap on the beat—but they were down front, grinning and trying.

> **When you put key leaders in visible places of leadership, people see and join in.**

When you put key leaders in visible places of leadership, people see and join in. This is one reason that a staff member should never do a job that others can do. When the people of your church see a staff member doing a job, they are not impressed. That is what they are paid to do. But when they see a lay person like themselves doing the job, they want to join in.

4. Put people to work where they are vested

Nehemiah knew that most of the people would have moderate interest in wanting to see the wall around the city rebuilt. He also reasoned that each person would be especially interested in seeing certain portions of the wall fixed. So when he put people to work rebuilding the wall, where did he assign them? He assigned them to the section closest to their house.

> *Benjamin and Hasshub made repairs **in front of their house** ... Azariah made repairs **beside his house** ... the priests made repairs **each in front of his own house** ... Meshukkam made repairs **opposite his living quarters**.*
>
> from Nehemiah 3:23–30

Put people to work where they are vested. There are three specific ways to do this. First, put them to work in areas that match their interests. The best youth workers in all the world are parents of youth. Why? Because they have a vested interest (their own kid) and because they have a current understanding of teens (or at least they know what they don't understand). Second, put them to work in areas where they have passion. I would rather have a worker with second-rate ability but first-rate passion than a worker with first-rate ability and no passion any day of the week. Passionless workers are more trouble than they are worth.

> Put them to work in areas that match their interests.... Put them to work in areas where they have passion....
> Put them to work in areas where they are already at work.

Third, put them to work in areas where they are already at work. We sometimes assume that the worker that succeeded in one arena can be moved to another where she is more needed. That is not always the case. Don't put square pegs in round holes. When you force them to fit, you knock off the edges that are a part of their God-given uniqueness. There are jobs in the church they can do well and there are jobs they cannot do at all based on their giftedness. Put them to work in areas where they are already proven. Promote them to a bigger job in that area before transferring them to something else outside their area of expertise.

Wrap up

How you implement your vision has much to do with whether or not your vision comes to pass. Be sure to implement your changes one at a time. Implement your changes in a strategic order (generally, purpose first, target second, and strategy changes last). Put your key leaders to work in visible places so that others can see that they are on board. Put people to work in places where they are vested (where they have an interest, a passion, or have already proven their effectiveness).

Key Truth: Build on your strengths, not your weaknesses.

Many churches try to program to their weaknesses rather than capitalizing on their God-given strengths. In an effort to encourage growth, they often add programs that they see working in other churches. In so doing, they often add

> **Most churches try to do too many things.**

ministries that they do not yet have leadership or capability to pull off. When we copy the strategy of other churches, we often wind up with programs and events that do not really fit the purpose and target of the church.

Most churches try to do too many things. They end up being a mile wide and an inch deep. At Flamingo Road Church, we major on three things: seeker sensitive weekend worship services, small group Bible study for every age group, and a believer oriented midweek worship service. Everything else that we do supports and complements these three main emphases.

Key Truth: You must go slow when implementing any changes related to vision.

Many churches make changes too fast. I get dozens of phone calls each month from pastors who have made the mistake of hurrying transition. Most of us can name churches that pushed transition through too hard and too fast. There is a right speed for the transition that you are trying to lead.

The speed of your transition is determined by four factors:

- **The distance you must go.** The farther you are going, the slower you must go. Small course corrections can be made fairly quickly. Complete turnarounds require more time.

- **The size of the ship.** The bigger the church, the slower you must go. Ski boats can turn in a few yards. It takes an oil tanker thirteen miles to turn around. Why? It's a big ship.

> God measures the size of a church by the size of its potential.

One sidebar here. I believe God measures the size of a church by the size of its potential. In other words, I believe God measures the size of your church the same way he measures the size of your giving. Remember the story in Luke 21 where Jesus is sitting where he can watch people put their money in the offering basket? He sees the rich folks put in their gifts. Then a poor widow puts in her last two coins. Jesus goes berserk. "Wow. Did you see that? She gave more than any of these guys!" (This is from the Southerland Revised Version). The disciples must have thought Jesus had been out in the sun too long. Then Jesus went on to explain that the rich had given large sums of money but had even more left for themselves. The poor widow had put in all she had to live on. In other words, God measures the size of our gift by what we still have left in our pockets after we have given.

I believe that God measures the size of our churches the same way—by our potential. I am often told that Flamingo Road is a large church. I could not disagree more. Flamingo Road is a small church. Last weekend we had 2100 in worship attendance. That's 2100 out of the 750,000 that live within a ten mile radius of our church. That means .28 percent—less than one third of one percent—of the people in our community attend our church. We are a small church.

Let me tell you about my grandmother's church in rural Oklahoma. For most of her eighty-five years, my grandmother attended the First Baptist Church of Velma, Oklahoma. That church averaged about 140 in worship attendance in a town of 400 and with a total population in the surrounding community of 1000. First Baptist Church was reaching 34 percent of its town and 14 percent of its total community. That is a large church. First Baptist Church Velma is a much bigger church than Flamingo Road in terms of reaching its community.

- **The age of the ship.** The older a church is, the slower you must go in implementing change. Flexibility belongs to the young. Younger churches usually have less tradition and more flexibility. Older churches tend to have more tradition and less flexibility. You can teach an old dog new tricks—but you must be really patient with the dog.

> You can teach an old dog new tricks—but you must be really patient with the dog.

- **The toughness of the leaders.** The tougher the leaders are who are implementing the change, the faster you can go. The problem is that many churches are led by insecure leaders who are more concerned about what people think than they need to be. The key is to be tough enough to lead the charge but gentle enough to care for the people who go up the hill with you. If you are not tough enough to take the heat, don't start the fire of leading a church through change.

> Many churches are led by insecure leaders who are more concerned about what people think than they need to be.

Go slow

Repeat after me: I will go slow, I will go slow, I will go slow. It cannot be said often enough: you must go slow when making transitions. If I had to give one overall contributing factor to our success in leading a traditional, program driven church for Christians to become a contemporary, purpose driven church for the unchurched it would be this: we took our sweet time. We actually enjoyed the journey.

At Flamingo Road, our transitions took four years:

- year one—we prepared for and defined the vision

- year two—we planted the vision with the leaders and shared it with the church

- year three—we began to implement smaller changes

- year four—we began to implement major changes

How long will your transitions take?

Step 1: Preparing for vision
Step 2: Defining the vision
Step 3: Planting the vision
Step 4: Sharing the vision
Step 5: Implementing the vision

Step 6

Dealing With Opposition

A learning exercise

When we teach this section of the vision process in our conferences, we start with an exercise. It goes like this. "Pair up with someone in the room. Face each other for a few seconds. Now turn back to back and change five things about your appearance." As you can imagine no one moves at first. Then glasses begin to come off, watches change hands, rings are removed, pens taken out of pockets. I then ask them to face each other and see if they can identify the five changes.

In phase two of this exercise I say, "Turn back to back again and change five different things about your appearance." Now they really have to think. Shirttails come out. Jackets or sweaters get removed. Sleeves get rolled up, socks get pushed down. I remember seeing one lady take her floor length skirt and make it knee length by pulling it up under her shoulders. Once again they face each other and identify the changes.

Phase three is where I say, "Now let's do it one more time!" A collective groan goes up from the crowd until we say, "Just kidding—please be seated."

Besides being a nice icebreaker, there are several lessons apparent in this exercise concerning how people deal with change:

- **People can only handle so much change.** They could have found five more things to change about their appearance—but they were tired of change.

- **People feel awkward when asked to do something new.** Most feel a bit self-conscious when asked to change. All change is new territory on the front end.

- **People think first about what they must give up.** I have done this exercise many times. People always begin by taking things off. Change can cause us to focus on what we are losing.

- **People feel alone when they are asked to change.** Even though they were not instructed to do this exercise on their own, I have never seen someone ask for help. Change tends to isolate us and make us think we are the only one going through it.

- **People are at different levels of readiness for change.** Some people enjoy this exercise while others hate it.

- **People tend to revert back to their old behavior the minute the reason to change is removed.** The minute this exercise is over, I watch the whole group put their jewelry back in place, tuck their shirttails back in, unroll their sleeves and re-button their buttons.

If there is that much resistance to a simple exercise, how much more resistance is coming to major transitions within the church?

The reality of opposition

If anyone in the Old Testament should have encountered no opposition, it was Nehemiah. He is trying to rebuild a wall that will make Jerusalem a safe place for all her inhabitants. His project will also regain a piece of Jerusalem's lost glory. The rebuilding of the wall will allow the people to once again worship in the temple without fear of their enemies. Everyone in town should be happy about Nehemiah's vision—right? Unfortunately, it does not work that way.

Anyone who is trying to do something for God will face some opposition. There is always opposition when you lead the church through transition. There will be opposition from those who do not understand the change. There will be opposition from those who understand the change but just don't like it. There will be opposition from those people whose kingdom you are messing with. There will be opposition from those people whom the enemy controls. There will be opposition from those people who just love to be contrary. You have each of these groups in your church.

> **Anyone who is trying to do something for God will face some opposition.**

This is another place in the process where the vision can get derailed quickly. Many of us are simply unprepared for the opposition that we get. So if opposition is coming—we need a plan to deal with it.

Two steps to take to deal with opposition

1. Expect opposition

Both of my grandmothers were wonderful, salt-of-the-earth women whom everyone loved. People were always stopping in unannounced. Since my grandmothers were phenomenal cooks (they are running the kitchen in heaven today, I am sure of it), people would generally manage to drop in pretty close to meal time. Both of these ladies had a great plan to handle unexpected guests: they always expected someone to just drop in. They prepared ahead because they knew more times than not company was coming—they just weren't sure which company it would be.

We must learn to expect the company of opposition to drop in when we are leading transition in the church. We cannot afford to be surprised when opposition shows up, even when we are surprised by who is bringing it.

The greatest difficulty with opposition is that it will discourage you and cause you to doubt your vision. If you are expecting it—you will be prepared.

> **The greatest difficulty with opposition is that it will discourage you and cause you to doubt your vision.**

Nehemiah's opposition

Nehemiah experienced five different kinds of opposition. We should expect no less.

Expect apathy. Some people just won't care about the vision. Nehemiah experienced this:

the nobles would not put their shoulders to the work under their supervisors.   Nehemiah 3:5b

Nehemiah had leaders who were apathetic. You will too. Some people are leaders because they are visionary. Some people are leaders because they are noisier and more opinionated than others. In other words, they are control freaks. (Many pastors I know fit into this camp.) Leaders who are control freaks will be apathetic toward your vision because they perceive it to be a lessening of their control.

In the early days of our transition, several of our leaders really struggled with apathy. One expressed his apathy in a theological smoke screen. The more I talked about seekers, the more apathetic he became. Finally he voiced his apathy out loud: "We don't need to worry about seekers; God is in charge of who gets saved." That may sound like a theological argument, but it came from a cold, apathetic heart that did not care about lost people. You will run into some apathy. It may be dressed up in theological clothes, but it is still just plain old apathy. Expect it.

Expect anger. Nehemiah's vision really ticked some people off:

> *When Sanballat heard that we were rebuilding the wall, he became angry and was greatly incensed.*   Nehemiah 4:1a

We all get mail from time to time that is less than complimentary of our ministries. But when you begin making major transitions in the church, that particular genre of mail increases greatly. I have received mail that has accused me of lying and of using psychology to manipulate the people of the church. I cannot even put in print some of the obscene names that I have been called. Some folks are going to get very angry. Expect it.

Expect ridicule. If you have read Nehemiah recently, you will remember that Sanballat is Nehemiah's greatest critic and number one enemy. Let me put it plainer than that. Sanballat is a leader from hell. I have not looked it up, but I am convinced that the Hebrew word for Sanballat means leader from hell.

We all have some Sanballats in our churches. This is the guy who opposes whatever you propose. The guy who hates whatever you like. The guy who wants to back up every time you want to move forward. You cannot call this guy a leader from hell to his face—but you could call him Sanballat.

Check out good old Sanballat: *"He ridiculed the Jews ..."* (*Nehemiah 4:1b*). The word for ridicule here literally means to trouble, to rage against, to be indignant toward. Modern forms would include mocking, making fun of, putting down, and being sarcastic.

You will get some ridicule. One form of ridicule that is popular today is name calling. A few of the names that have been thrown at us are liberal, heretic, new ager, manipulator, and false prophet (and those are just the names I get called in staff meetings). Get the picture? You better expect some ridicule.

Expect criticism. Sanballat is still at it. The leader from hell is trying to prevail. Look at his next tirade:

> *"What are those feeble Jews doing? Will they restore their wall? ... What are they building—if even a fox climbed up on it, he would break down their wall of stones."*   Nehemiah 4:2–3

Sanballat is saying, "This isn't going to work. You guys can't pull this thing off. Even if you do, it won't last."

Some people are going to be critical. This reminds me of a story I heard about a family who had been to church together. On the drive home they were critiquing the worship service. The dad said, "The sermon was long." The mom said, "The music was boring." The teenager added, "The whole thing was long and boring." Then the five year old chirped in, "I thought it was a pretty good show for a buck."

We have experienced two major sources of criticism during our transitions. The first is Christians from more traditional backgrounds. They sometimes struggle with transitions in the church. Not all of our traditional backgrounded Christians have been critical—just the ornery ones. Our second source of criticism is traditional church pastors. Again, not all traditional church pastors—just the meaner ones. I believe that is because they do not understand what we are doing. I hope it is not out of jealousy of our results. Your sources of criticism may differ from ours, but you will be criticized. Expect it.

Expect a fight. If you think your opposition will go away without a fight, think again. There is a fight coming. Notice what Nehemiah's opposition group is up to:

> **If you think your opposition will go away without a fight, think again.**

> *They all plotted together to come and fight against Jerusalem and stir up trouble against it.*   *Nehemiah 4:8*

They were not planning an out in the open frontal attack. They were trying to infiltrate the ranks:

"Before they know it or see us, we will be right there among them and will kill them and put an end to the work."

Nehemiah 4:11

Our OK Corral–style shoot-out came during a deacon's meeting. One deacon decided it was time to confront me in front of twenty other deacons. He had not been to me one-on-one, but he was not interested in being biblical. So in a two minute explosion, he said that I had quit preaching the gospel, that I did not care that people were leaving the church, and that the new music we were doing was awful. He concluded his outburst with a statement: "We need to go back to the way we used to do church!"

Three things happened next. One of our pastors spoke up in my defense. The other deacons spoke up. And I stood my ground. I said, "This is where I have to go. I must do church for the unchurched; I can't go back to doing church for the already convinced. If you want to go with me, please do." We then reviewed our purpose, target, and strategy as a group. And I lived to fight another day. There will be a show down somewhere along the way. Expect it.

Key Truth: Don't take criticism personally.

That is so easy to say and so hard to do. It is especially hard for those of us who are people pleasers by nature—which I am. I am a die-hard people pleaser. I want everyone to be happy. I love to say "yes" and hate to say "no" to anyone. So I tend to take criticism very personally.

I discovered a truth years ago that has really helped me. You will be criticized regardless of what you do—so you might as well be criticized for doing what God wants you to do. Isn't

> ## You will be criticized. It might as well be for doing the right thing.

that true? You will be criticized. So it might as well be for doing the right thing.

Paul understood this truth:

> *Am I now trying to win the approval of men, or of God? Or am I trying to please men? If I were still trying to please men, I would not be a servant of Christ.*   *Galatians 1:10*

That verse says that you must choose your audience!

The reality of criticism

These three statements about criticism have really set us free at Flamingo Road to pursue what God wants to do:

- **You cannot please everyone.** Jesus didn't—and you and I won't either.

- **You cannot please anyone all the time.** Anyone who has been married more than five minutes knows that.

- **You can please God.** He is much easier to please than people.

So choose your audience. One of our favorite phrases here at Flamingo Road is *"play to an audience of One."* Remember who your final and most important audience is going to be.

Don't be surprised by opposition and criticism. Expect it. Don't let it sneak up on you and catch you off guard. If you don't expect it, you can be trapped by the greatest difficulty of opposition: you will become discouraged and doubt your vision.

2. Keep on track

The second great difficulty with opposition is that it can distract you and drain you. It draws your attention away from the main thing to side issues. It causes you to become consumed with the urgent rather than the important. You become a church fireman rather than a church builder.

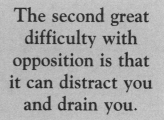

The second great difficulty with opposition is that it can distract you and drain you.

The key then is to keep on track. If you get offtrack, the vision is offtrack. If the enemy can get the main visionary and the main vision team offtrack, he has successfully derailed the entire vision.

Nehemiah's track record

Nehemiah must have known that opposition could cause him to get distracted from his vision. He kept on track in five specific ways that will work for us as well.

Keep on praying. By chapter four the opposition that Nehemiah is facing is really high. Here is his first response:

> *Hear us, O our God, for we are despised. Turn their insults back on their heads ... for they have thrown their insults in the face of the builders.* Nehemiah 4:4–5

Have you ever noticed that those who are builders are always being criticized by those who refuse to work! My tendency is to do everything I can to fix the opposition first and to rely on prayer as my last resort. Nehemiah's first response to opposition was prayer.

> The reality is that criticism and opposition will drive you somewhere. Let it drive you closer to God and you will become better; let it drive you away from God and you will become bitter.

Prayer is vital in the vision process. Prayer fuels your vision, ignites your vision, and preserves your vision. The reality is that criticism and opposition will drive you somewhere. Let it drive you closer to God and you will become better; let it drive you away from God and you will become bitter. The choice is up to you! And the choice often begins with prayer.

One of the key ingredients in our successful transitions is the commitment of our mature Christians in the church to prayer. They have prayed for us as we have made tough decisions. They have prayed for us as we have gone through personal difficulties. They have prayed for us to keep seeking God and to not give in to the skeptics. There is even a group that is praying for me now as I am writing this script. Ask your people to pray. And whatever you do—you keep on praying.

Keep on working. One of the real dangers of opposition is that it can immobilize you. Anyone who gets down tends to slow down—it is a fact of life. If we stay discouraged and depressed long enough, we may actually shut down all

> Anyone who gets down tends to slow down— it is a fact of life.

together. When the train of vision totally shuts down, it is difficult to get it moving again.

So keep on working when you are faced with opposition. Even when the criticism was at its highest, Nehemiah kept on working. He refused to be distracted.

So we rebuilt the wall till all of it reached its height, for the people worked with all their heart. Nehemiah 4:6

I live in South Florida where hurricanes are a fact of life. We had several years without a major storm, and people tended to become lax about their preparation. When hurricane Andrew hit in 1992, all that changed. Now we are much more aware of what a hurricane can do, and we have gone to the other extreme. Last week we had a hurricane warning. Two days before the storm could possibly arrive, everything began shutting down. Schools, businesses, churches, doctor's offices— even Wal-Mart! It was eerie. The storm was clearly going to miss our area, but it came close enough that everyone overreacted and put their lives on hold for two whole days. If this trend continues, every summer and fall for the next ten years will see a down turn in productivity in South Florida— because there is always a storm just offshore this time of year!

The same thing tends to happen in church. We all can remember the havoc that the last internal storm caused in the church. So when we see another one brewing, we shut down whatever work is going on and ride out the storm. The reality

> There is always a potential storm brewing somewhere out there.

is that there is always a potential storm brewing somewhere out there. We must change our mentality from being riders on the storm to that of choosing to be workers through the storm.

The temptation when you know a storm is coming is to say "the opposition is too heavy and too hot—let's quit working for a while and let this blow over." If the enemy can see that you will shut down every time a threatening cloud comes by, he will keep your skies just dark enough to keep you immobile. Stay at it. Keep on working.

Keep on encouraging. I never have been very good at spelling. I thank God regularly for a wife who can proofread and a computer with spell check. I misspell many words and don't have a clue that I messed up. (I do believe that it is a narrow mind that can spell a word only one way.)

There is one word that I deliberately misspell on a regular basis. It is the word "encourage." I spell it with an "I"— "incourage." That helps me to remember what encourage means: to put courage in someone. Literally, that means to "in courage" them—"incourage."

Nehemiah went out of his way to "incourage" his troops in the midst of opposition:

> *After I looked things over, I stood up and said to the nobles, the officials and the rest of the people, "Don't be afraid of them. Remember the Lord, who is great and awesome, and fight for your brothers and sons and daughters, your wives and your homes."*   Nehemiah 4:14

Nehemiah "incouraged" the people by saying three things. First, don't be afraid of your critics. Second, remember that your God is on your side. Third, remember your purpose. (Sounds like a good sermon outline to me.)

If you have been battling with discouragement, I would like to say three things to you.

- **First, don't be afraid of your critics.** You cannot control what they say or do. You can control your response to them. They will answer to God for what they say about you. You will answer to God for how you respond.

- **Second, remember that God is with you.** I love what Paul tells us in Romans 8:31b: *"If God is for us, who can be against us?"* Is that a great verse or what? I have my own translation of that verse written into the margin of my Bible: *"If God is for us, who cares who is against us?"* (Revised Southerland Perversion) When Elisha faced a whole army of opposition he responded *"Don't be afraid ... those who are with us are more than those who are with them"* (2 Kings 6:16).

- **Third, remember your purpose.** If the quest you are on is to complete your vision, you should be afraid of your critics. But if your purpose is to complete God's vision, then be "incouraged" and stay on track.

Jerry Falwell says, "You can define the greatness of a man by what it takes to discourage him." Keep on incouraging.

Keep on leading. One of the ways opposition distracts us is it moves our focus from those we are leading to those we cannot lead. It causes us to take our attention away from

> **"You can define the greatness of a man by what it takes to discourage him."**

those who are working and give it to those who are opposing. Notice how Nehemiah addressed this issue:

> *The officers posted themselves behind all the people of Judah who were building the wall.*   Nehemiah 4:16b

Nehemiah brought all his leaders out from their work as behind the scenes planners and put them with the people who were working on the wall. He knew that the people needed to see two things: that their leaders were with them and that their leaders were still leading.

It is impossible to lead the team up the hill when you are constantly giving your time and attention to those who refuse to join the charge. If your people see that you have quit leading, they will quit following. You must continue to give your time to that which is important—not just that which seems urgent.

> **It is impossible to lead the team up the hill when you are constantly giving your time and attention to those who refuse to join the charge.**

During one of our more tumultuous stretches, I was reporting to a group of leaders on all the critics that I had been meeting with to try to win them over. After quite a list, one of the leaders responded, "It seems to me that the way to get some time with you is to be a troublemaker." Ouch! He was right. I had fallen into the trap of spending all my time and attention on those who were not following rather than leading those who were following.

Part of my learning curve during that time was a teaching (he calls them "talks") that I heard Bill Hybels give at a Willow

Creek Church Leadership Conference. Hybels said, "You only have enough tears for one group: those who are walking toward you or those who are walking away from you. Choose whom you will weep over." Did you get it? I got it. Here is the translation. Don't let the whiners set the agenda of your church. Don't let the complainers have the time that you need to be giving to the work-ers. Don't get so trapped behind the lines with those who refuse to march forward that you forget to lead those who are on the front line in the midst of the battle. Keep on leading.

> **Don't let the whiners set the agenda of your church. Don't let the complainers have the time that you need to be giving to the workers.**

Keep on watching. You must stay alert to stay on track. Jesus told us to *"be wise as serpents and as gentle as doves"* (Matthew 10:16, NKJ). Jesus also warned us to watch out for the false prophets who were really *"wolves in sheep's clothing"* (Matthew 7:15). Anytime you are doing something for God, the wolves in sheep's clothing will be gathering. Wolves always gather to prey on the youngest and weakest lambs in the flock. And never forget—wolves hunt in packs. They love to group up before they attack. We had one group that met every week for six months to pray that we would see the error of our ways and return the church to its former condition. In reality, they were not meeting to pray—they were meeting to plan their attack.

If you are of the opinion that you are over the hump and that the opposition has dispersed and fled, think again. Time and time again I have decided that once this wave of opposition is over, it will let up. Wrong. The good news is that the waves of opposition seem to be fewer and farther in between at this point in our journey at Flamingo Road. The bad news is there is always a wave stirring up somewhere.

Wolves rarely leave the area. They are still out there lurking in the darkness, waiting for you to doze off at your post. That is why Nehemiah made this decree:

> *"Have every man and helper stay inside Jerusalem at night, so they can serve as guards by night and workmen by day."*
> *Nehemiah 4:22b*

What a great balance! We are to be "guards by night" when the attack is most likely to come and "workmen by day" when it's time to put your hands to the work. Peter reminds us of the importance of watching: *"Be shepherds of God's flock that is under your care, serving as overseers ..."* (1 Peter 5:2a). If we are wise, we will keep on watching.

Wrap up

It is a physical law of the universe that all moving objects encounter resistance. The only object that encounters no opposition is one that is stationary.

> **All moving objects encounter resistance.**

When you begin to implement God's vision in the church, you will encounter opposition. The first step to dealing with it is to expect it. Apathy, anger, ridicule, criticism, and fights may all come your way. The second step to surviving opposition is to stay on track. You must choose to keep on praying, working, encouraging, leading, and watching—even when everything in you wants to quit. Remember what James told us about keeping on:

*Dear brothers, is your life full of difficulties and temptations?
Then be happy, for when the way is rough, your patience has
a chance to grow. So let it grow, and don't try to squirm out of
your problems. For when your patience is finally in full bloom,
then you will be ready for anything, strong in character, full
and complete.*   *James 1:2–4* (TLB)

Key Truth: Be willing to let people leave the church.

Please take careful note of
what I am about to say. The
reality of ministry is this: people will leave your church no
matter what you do. That is
the nature of the beast. One
of the hardest parts of ministry is when people you have
poured your life into leave the
church. But when you set the
vision and stay the course,
you determine who leaves.

> We lost three
> hundred people—and
> gained two thousand.
> We have lost three
> hundred who were
> already committed to
> Christ—and gained
> two thousand, most
> of whom were
> unchurched.

When I share about our transitions at Flamingo Road, I am
invariably asked, "Did you lose any people as you made your
transitions?" What do you think? Yes! As far as we can tell, we
have lost about 300 people over the last nine years who could
not handle our changes. About half of the original 300 people who were here when we began our transitions have left us
over the years; others that came on board as we were changing later left when we continued to transition. We have lost
300 people—and gained 2,000. We have lost three hundred
that were already committed to Christ—and gained two thousand, most of whom were unchurched, lost, and going to hell.
Do you ever want to lose people whom you love? No. But

would we take this swap again today if it were offered to us? In a skinny minute.

By the way—almost all of the 300 who have left us have found other church homes. Many of them are now a part of the sixteen mission churches we have started. They are not at Flamingo Road—but they are still in the family. They have not been lost to the kingdom. In fact, most of them are much more productive where they are now than they ever were at Flamingo Road—because now they are in churches where they can give their wholehearted support.

Let me close this chapter with a story. Bob (not his real name; there is a slight chance he might read this someday) was a long-term member of Flamingo Road. As far as I can tell, all he ever did while he was here was gripe and grumble. Bob and I had a couple of run-ins, and I challenged him about his critical spirit. He eventually left us and went to a small mission church in our area.

I ran into Bob a couple of years later in a local restaurant on my way to the airport to lead a conference. I knew something was up when he shook my hand and said, "It's good to see you." He then proceeded to tell me how much he loved his church. He was more actively involved than ever before. He was teaching a Bible study class and had just been asked to serve as a deacon. Bob was being a productive church member and a supportive leader—two things he never did at Flamingo Road.

Later that day on the airplane, I had a moment to reflect on my encounter in the restaurant. Bob was happy—because he was being productive. I was happy—because Bob was no longer poisoning his friends at Flamingo Road. God was happy—because two of his churches are now in better shape. That is a win-win-win circumstance. Go God!

Step 1: Preparing for vision
Step 2: Defining the vision
Step 3: Planting the vision
Step 4: Sharing the vision
Step 5: Implementing the vision
Step 6: Dealing with opposition

Step 7

Making Course Corrections

Vision is a journey

The Southerland clan spent the summer vacation of 1996 making our longest car trip yet. We traveled from Fort Lauderdale to North Carolina, stayed a week, then drove up through the Amish country of Pennsylvania and toured New York City on our way to upstate New York. The journey home included a swing through Ohio to see the Pro Football Hall of Fame and at least a hundred stops at outlet malls along the way. All told we logged 5100 miles on the old Dodge Caravan. According to my twelve-year-old daughter Danna, who is the life of our party, this trip was "really cool."

I love trips. But I love planning trips almost as much as taking them. I spend hours with my Atlas. I have a Road Whiz that tells me what fast food and gas options are available on the way. I keep a map showing the locations of my favorite restaurant, the Cracker Barrel, in my car at all times. Before we ever get in the car I know the exact mileages, the exact route, the exact plan.

This trip, however, did not go according to my plans. It was full of detours. Some of the roads were under construction. Some were shut down all together. Others were just not as good as they looked on the map. We did, in fact, make it to all the places we planned—and lived to tell about it. But we had to make constant adjustments along the way.

Trips are like that. Life is like that. Vision is like that. The process of transitioning a church to a purpose driven model is a major journey. Every step requires course corrections along the way. So the challenge is to learn as you go and make the necessary changes along the way. Only a fool does not learn as he makes his journey. The only thing more painful than learning from experience is not learning from experience.

Nehemiah's course corrections

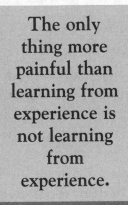

The only thing more painful than learning from experience is not learning from experience.

Nehemiah may have been surprised at the course corrections he had to make. His vision is in place. The wall is going up. The opposition has been dealt with for the moment. The journey is well under way and the end is in sight. Yet exactly halfway through his project—the rebuilding of the wall—he has to stop and make three course corrections.

Nehemiah's course corrections are certainly not the only possible challenges we will face as we lead transition. But the likelihood is that we will face these course corrections and even more at some point in the transition process.

1. Care for the neglected

Any time a church goes through major changes, someone feels neglected. It is not that hard to tell if this is in fact happening in your church. Neglected people usually let you know by complaining. Nehemiah's neglected people spoke up:

> *Now the men and their wives raised a great outcry against their Jewish brothers.*   *Nehemiah 5:1*

It is important to note that this is not criticism that is coming from outside the camp. These are complaints that are coming from within. The concerns voiced here are coming from teammates, from fellow workers.

Nehemiah's complainers

Closer analysis reveals that Nehemiah had at least three groups that were complaining.

- **The "this is too hard" group.** Even among good work crews, there are some who struggle with the toughness of the work.

  > *Some were saying, "We and our sons and daughters are numerous; in order for us to eat and stay alive, we must get grain."*   *Nehemiah 5:2*

  Those with the larger families had a problem. The work on the wall was so time and energy consuming that they were struggling to feed their own families. The work was hard.

  Transitions are always hard work, and some of the work crew is going to let you know how hard it is.

- **The "price is too high" group.** There is a price to be paid for vision.

> *Others were saying, "We are mortgaging our fields, our vineyards and our homes to get grain during the famine."*
> Nehemiah 5:3

It was hard enough to try to balance working on the wall and caring for your family. To make matters worse, there was a famine going in the land. These people are really paying a high price.

> There is always a price for transition. And there are always those who think the price is too high.

There is always a price for transition. And there are always those who think the price is too high.

- **The "this is not fair" group.** Nehemiah had some folks who were feeling they were not being treated fairly.

> *"Although we are of the same flesh and blood as our countrymen and though our sons are as good as theirs, yet we have to subject our sons and daughters to slavery."*
> Nehemiah 5:5a

Here's the deal: some of Nehemiah's folks are saying, "We can't afford to work on the wall—we have to work to feed our families." Others are saying, "We have mortgaged our homes and farms and fields just to be able to live." Another group jumps in with, "We are borrowing money just to pay our taxes." This last group complains, "That's nothing—we had to sell our kids off as laborers just to make ends meet." (This is an idea most parents have considered at some point.) It almost seems that most of Nehemiah's workers feel they are being mistreated.

The reality of any transition is that it is harder on some than it is on others. That is simply the nature of transition. If you change the music in worship to a more contemporary style, the younger crowd will like it better than the more traditional crowd. If you change the function of deacons from decision makers to servants, those who loved being in charge are going to feel it is unfair while those who are more comfortable in serving will love it. The very nature of change means that it is going to feel unfair to someone.

Nehemiah had people that were feeling left out, overlooked, and mistreated. He had some workers who were not happy campers. You probably will too!

> The very nature of change means that it is going to feel unfair to someone.

Possible responses to complainers

I truly believe that you can measure a leader's maturity by how he responds to complainers. There are at least three possible responses.

- **First possible response to complainers: dismiss them as troublemakers who just like to complain.** There really are some people in the world who just like to complain. They were born nasty and got worse. They are professional troublemakers who love to stir things up. They aren't happy unless someone else is upset. My dad says, "You couldn't please some people if you hung them with a new rope."

To dismiss the complaint is the right response if it is coming from someone who believes that complaining is a virtue. It is the right response if the complaint is not legitimate because it is coming from a divisive person.

> **You can measure a leader's maturity by how he responds to complainers.**

> *Warn a divisive person once, and then warn him a second time. After that, have nothing to do with him. Titus 3:10*

Those are pretty strong words. Warn a divisive person once. Warn them a second time. Then ignore him! Dismissing the complaint is the right response if it comes from a proven troublemaker.

But dismissing the complainer is the wrong response if his complaint is legitimate. He may have a concern that needs to be addressed, or his cry may simply be coming from the heart of a wounded person. So we must slow down long enough to discern what is taking place so we can choose our response wisely.

Nehemiah was wise enough to slow down his response. Notice how different translations record his actions in Nehemiah 5:6-7a:

> *When I heard their outcry and these charges, I was very angry. **I pondered them in my mind.** (NIV)*

> *"And I became very angry when I heard their outcry and these words. **After serious thought**.... (NKJ)*

*I was very angry when I heard this; so **after thinking about it I spoke out**.* (TLB)

*And I was very angry when I heard their cry and these words. **Then I consulted with myself**.* (ASV)

Nehemiah was furious when he first heard their complaints. But he was wise enough to ponder them in his mind, give them serious thought, and take his time before giving his response. He measured his words very carefully.

Jesus modeled this same behavior for us when he finds the temple full of thieves. He took the time to braid a whip to use to drive them out—probably to have time to calm down and choose his words (see John 2:13–16).

The angrier you are about a complaint, the more sensitive you need to be in your response. Don't just dismiss those who complain as people who love to make trouble. Take the time to see if the complaint is legitimate. You may discover that their complaint is simply the expression of a deeper wound.

> **The angrier you are about a complaint, the more sensitive you need to be in your response.**

- **Second possible response to complainers: discount them as people who do not understand your vision.** There will be some people in your church who do not understand your vision. For some, it may be they do not want to understand it. For others, it may be because they cannot understand it. I am convinced that some people cannot think in visionary terms. I spoke earlier of the fact that vision is caught like a cold; you must be around someone who is contagious. Some people cannot catch vision even when they are exposed to it repeatedly. They are vision immune. They have vision antibodies in their system. Maybe they got a vision vaccination through some experience in another church. They just can't catch it. There are some people in your church who do not or cannot understand your vision. But it is a mistake to assume that this is true of everyone who complains.

Nehemiah's complainers were from all across his work force. If he had dismissed all of the people who ever complained, he would have failed because there would have been no one left to carry out the vision. He was wise enough to listen:

> *I heard their outcry and these charges.*   Nehemiah 5:6a

Don't shoot your wounded people just because they are complaining. It is normal for people who are hurt to cry out. If you start shooting your wounded, you will soon have no one left, because we all are wounded in some way or another at some time or another. Everyone complains once in a while.

> **Don't shoot your wounded people just because they are complaining.**

We need to remember that the church is not a museum for perfect saints; it is a hospital for wounded sinners. I once had a lady tell me that she was looking for a perfect church. Although I realized that she was half kidding, I said, "Ma'am, when you find it, please don't join. You'll just mess it up." Those churches who think they are museums for perfect saints are very empty: only people who think they are perfect want to come. One of our pastors told me of seeing a church sign that read "only mature Christians

> **The church is not a museum for perfect saints; it is a hospital for wounded sinners.**

wanted." We are not after the"already mature" crowd at Flamingo Road; we are after the "pagan as they come" group. Those churches that hang out their shingle as a hospital for wounded sinners are full—because the world is full of wounded people. David Foster, who is the pastor of the Bellvue Community Church in Nashville, Tennessee says that his church is known as "the church where all the screwups go." He takes that as a compliment. I agree.

You can respond to complainers by dismissing them as troublemakers. You can respond to complainers by writing them off as people who do not understand your vision.

- **Third possible response to complainers: demonstrate your care for them by making a plan to provide for their needs.** Nehemiah did not just commiserate with their complaints. When he concluded that they were legitimate, he acted:

> *So I called together a large meeting to deal with them.*
> *Nehemiah 5:7b*

This was not just a meeting for the sake of meeting. First Nehemiah corrected those who were out of line. He also made the people follow through with their commitments. When he had finished, the complaints were dealt with and unity had been restored.

At this the whole assembly said "Amen," and praised the Lord. And the people did as they promised.
                                                          Nehemiah 5:13b

It is important to take the time in the midst of major transition to care for those who have legitimate concerns and are being neglected. It is easy during times of change for people to feel that they are not loved. In the midst of our transitions at Flamingo Road, one group who felt a bit neglected was our senior adults. As we begin to grow and to change our style of worship, they felt a bit left out. Truth is, they were getting less time and attention from the staff.

> It is easy during times of change for people to feel that they are not loved.

A major change occurred that God used in a big way. We turned the senior ministry over to a senior adult deacon. Lincoln Love was his name. He was a white-headed, eighty-plus-year-old ball of fire. Lincoln began to care for the widow ladies. He drove them back and forth to the doctor and made sure they had a ride to church. Lincoln and his wife Marion began taking the widows to dinner on Friday nights. Soon this group of widows were laughingly calling themselves "Lincoln's Harem." (Just because there is snow on the roof does not mean there is no fire in the fireplace.) Lincoln has since gone on to be with the Lord, and other faithful senior deacons have taken his place. Our seniors get better care and more attention today than they ever got from the staff.

Demonstrating your care does not always mean that you must do all the caring. Sometimes it means that you must make sure that the caring gets done. Nehemiah's first course correction was to care for the neglected.

2. Negotiate peace

Nehemiah had to take the time to negotiate peace among his people. His workers were divided into camps and were complaining against each other. So he took action to negotiate a peace:

"What you are doing is not right. Shouldn't you walk in the fear of our God to avoid the reproach of our enemies?"
Nehemiah 5:9

There is a pivotal moment in most transitions where peace must be waged. It is that moment when war is about to break out among your people. I cannot tell you when it will occur, but I can tell you where to look for it. You will likely have to stop and negotiate peace among one or more of these groups:

> There is a pivotal moment in most transitions where peace must be waged.

• **Between those who like the changes and those who do not.** You will have some in both camps, and they will tend to be vocal about it.

• **Between those who are involved and those who feel left out.** The buy-in rate for vision is always higher among those who are in the trenches. The troops along the front lines seem to have a better sense for what needs to be done. Those who are doing the work will be the quickest to buy in. Those who prefer to sit and talk will be the slowest. However, the sitters will be the quickest to feel neglected.

- **Between the old guard leaders who are resisting the changes and the new guard leaders who are on board.** It is amazing how many times God raises up new leadership when He wants to do a new thing. This can lead to conflict. The leaders who have been there the longest—especially the ones who have been there longer than you—will be among the slowest to buy in. The new leaders God has raised up—especially those who have come after you—will be among the quickest to buy in.

> It is amazing how many times God raises up new leadership when He wants to do a new thing.

The next time you think you have leadership problems, remember Nehemiah. He had leaders who would not work (nobles in 3:5), leaders who were taking advantage of the workers (officials in 5:7), leaders who were fully against him (Sanballat and Tobiah in 4:1–3), and some leaders who were fully on board (the priests working on the gates in 3:1). His leaders were all across the spectrum. He had no choice but to negotiate peace. Chances are you will have to do the same. So get out the old peace pipe, or the cigars, or whatever works. Be ready to negotiate peace.

Nehemiah's course corrections included caring for those who felt neglected and negotiating peace.

3. Stay among the people

This is important stuff. Let me give you some history to show you why. Since the conquest of Jerusalem, the city had been ruled by appointed governors who lived a life of luxury. While the people struggled with poverty and while the city lay in ruins, these governors enjoyed the good life. They stayed in the governor's mansion. They received a huge food allowance, even during times of famine while the people were hungry. They collected a large salary. They had a big staff of servants.

These earlier governors collected heavy taxes from the people to support their luxurious lifestyle. They lived a lifestyle far above the people of the city—and they even flaunted it.

> *The earlier governors ... placed a heavy burden on the people and took forty shekels of silver from them in addition to the food and wine. Their assistants also lorded it over the people.*
> *Nehemiah 5:15a*

This is the context that Nehemiah inherited. He received the same appointment as these former governors. So when he showed up, the people were not too excited.

Nehemiah's edge

Although his appointment was the same as the governors that preceded him, Nehemiah was cut from a different cloth. His behavior was markedly different. He chose to stay among his people. He was one of them. How did he do that?

- **He did not take the royal food allowance.** There was a famine in the land when Nehemiah arrived in the city (see Nehemiah 5:1–3). For Nehemiah to take food and wine from every family when they did not have enough to feed their own would have been more than just wrong; it would have killed his vision before it got started. So he refused the food allowance.

> *Neither I nor my brothers ate the food allotted to the governor.*
> *Nehemiah 5:14c*

• **He shared his table with leaders, visitors, and any commoners who were hungry.** Not only did Nehemiah refuse to take food from the people; he shared what he had with them. Rather than taking from them, he gave to them:

> *Furthermore, a hundred and fifty Jews and officials ate at my table, as well as those who came to us from surrounding nations.*   *Nehemiah 5:17*

One hundred and fifty dinner guests—on a regular basis. That's what I call having company for dinner!

• **He treated his people with dignity and respect.** For decades before him, the governors had treated the people as slaves. Nehemiah treated them as people of value. He understood that people matter to God—so they mattered to him.

> *But the earlier governors ... [and] their assistants lorded it over the people. But out of reverence for God I did not act like that.*   *Nehemiah 5:15*

• **He cared for his people.** The former governors saw the people as property to be used. Nehemiah saw them as people to be loved.

> *I never demanded the food allotted to the governor, because the demands were heavy on these people.*
> *Nehemiah 5:18b*

• **He worked on the wall beside the people.** This had to be one of the most amazing sights of all. The people had never even seen the governor's staff work, much less the governor.

I devoted myself to the work on this wall. All my men were assembled for the work. Nehemiah 5:16

Nehemiah stayed among his people. He knew that to lead them, he had to be one of them.

Ways we separate ourselves from our people

Some of you who are reading this book have agreed with everything I have said to this point. I need to fix that. Think with me

> **People are not looking for a pastor who is a doctor. They are looking for a pastor who is a person.**

about some of the ways that we as church leaders (and especially as church staff) separate ourselves from our people. Let me make some suggestions.

- **Titles.** Titles like "Dr. Dan Southerland." I have 150 credit hours of graduate education. That's 150 hours beyond the bachelor's degree. That includes a master's, a Ph.D., and most of a second masters and most of a second Ph.D. I have the graduate schooling of a medical doctor. But no one calls me doctor. I don't use that title. Why? Because people are not looking for a pastor who is a doctor. They are looking for a pastor who is a person.

I love the way James records the story of Elijah praying for rain. Elijah prayed that it would not rain in Israel and it in fact did not rain for three and a half years. Then he prayed that it would rain and it did. In the midst of recording this account, James writes that *"Elijah was a man just like us" (James 5:17a)*. That is the most impressive part of the story to me; Elijah was an ordinary guy with extraordinary faith.

> If you have to have a title to have their respect, you still don't have their respect even with the title.

The people in our church don't call me Dr. Southerland. They know me too well to call me reverend. A few still call me pastor, although that is confusing because we have seven pastors on our staff. Most just call me Dan.

Titles separate us. If you have to have a title to have their respect, you still don't have their respect even with the title.

- **Dress.** How we dress can separate us. Why do pastors outdress their people? The pastors on the staff at Flamingo Road wore suits to worship for years. One day as we were beginning to reach unchurched people, we looked out and noticed something. The only people in the worship service who were wearing suits were the staff and visitors from other churches. The seekers and most of our church people were in casual attire. So we quit wearing suits. I don't even have one anymore. I still have a sports jacket in my closet, but the suits and ties are long gone. (Personally I am convinced that suits and ties were invented in hell in the first place—so I am glad to be free of them!)

> If you are dressing up for church, who are you trying to impress?

Dress separates us. If you are dressing up for church, who are you trying to impress? Remember what God said about outward appearances:

> *The Lord does not look at the things man looks at. Man looks at the outward appearance, but the Lord looks at the heart.* 1 Samuel 16:7b

Our statement at Flamingo Road is "dress is irrelevant." If you want to dress up for church, go for it. If you want to dress down, that's fine as well. Just dress!

- **Language and volume of speech.** If you pray in public in King James English, you are about to be offended. Why do people do that? Is it for God—because he only understands four-hundred-year-old English? It is clearly not for those who are listening as you pray—they certainly do not understand four-hundred-year-old English. Why do we do that? If you launch into fancy language when you speak, who are you trying to impress?

I am already in trouble here so I might as well go for it. Why are we using a Bible that is written in four-hundred-year old English when there are multiple translations out today that are trustworthy? The Bible is hard enough to understand without us complicating it by insisting that people read it in Shakespearean English. I studied MacBeth in high school English. The only way I made it was with Cliff Notes. MacBeth was written in the same year and in the same language as the King James.

> The only two places in our country today where a baby boomer gets yelled at are in a traffic jam and at church.

Volume of speech is another way we separate ourselves from people. If you get loud, may I ask you why? That style of preaching made sense a generation ago, but today we have this wonderful invention called a microphone. The only two places in our country today where a baby boomer gets yelled at are in a traffic jam and at church.

The world is looking for a Christian who is normal

Titles separate us, dress separates us, language and volume of speech separate us. Do I even need to tell you what I think about reserved parking places for the staff and putting the senior pastor's name on the church sign?

> Your community is looking for Christian leaders who are real.

Please hear my heart. Your community is looking for Christian leaders who are real. They are looking for Christian leaders who are not odd for God. They are looking for Christian leaders who are normal people with an abnormal commitment to Jesus Christ. When they find those kind of leaders—regular people who love God—they will flock to them.

Two leadership styles

When it comes to vision, there are two possible styles of leadership. The first is *ex-cathedra leadership*, which literally means "from on high." This is "lord it over them" leadership. It is dictatorship, and even benevolent dictatorship is still dictatorship. The second choice is *ex-comradre leadership*, which literally means to lead "from within." This is servant leadership. This is what Jesus modeled.

Martyrs versus leaders

Do you know the difference between a martyr and a leader? The difference is two steps. A martyr is three steps in front of his people. Your people will get so frustrated trying to keep up with you that they will want to shoot you ... in the back! A leader is one step in front of his people. He is close enough to them to still be one of them, and in front enough to still be the leader.

Wrap up

There are some course corrections that must be made along the way as you lead the church through transition. Possibilities will include caring for the neglected who are complaining, negotiating peace among various factions, and staying among the people.

Key Truth: Continually remind people why you are changing.

> **People need to hear vision again and again until it becomes a part of their soul.**

The drift is always downward in the vision process. That means that we tend to drift away from our defined purpose, target, and strategy. We forget what it is that we are doing, who it is that we are trying to reach, and why we are doing it this way. People need to hear vision again and again until it becomes a part of their soul. They need to hear it until it becomes their vision—and then they will still need to hear it so they won't forget. Keep reminding people why you are changing. To be purpose driven, you must keep purpose, target, and strategy in front of people on a continual basis.

Key Truth: Continually affirm and appreciate people for the changes they are making.

The old saying is *"You get what you encourage."* Brag on people when they change. Affirm their flexibility every time they display it. We have actually succeeded in creating a climate of change at Flamingo Road Church. We have made so many changes that people now expect it. The first question I am asked at our monthly leadership team meeting is "What are we changing next?" The issue is no longer "Will Flamingo Road make the needed change?" The only issue now is "Which change do we need to make?"

I am often asked why the people of Flamingo Road are willing to change. There are many reasons. One of them is that we brag on them. The pastors often say to the people something like this: "We want to thank you for being the most unselfish church we know. You have been willing to give up your style of worship for us to use a contemporary style that draws the young adults of this community. You have been willing to move to the Saturday night worship services so that a seeker can have your seat on Sunday morning. You have been willing to give of your time and your talent and your treasure so we can reach people for Christ. You have been willing to do whatever it takes. We are proud to be your pastors and would rather be here with you than in any other church in the world."

When you catch people doing something right and brag on them, they will go the second mile to do it again.

Step 1: Preparing for vision
Step 2: Defining the vision
Step 3: Planting the vision
Step 4: Sharing the vision
Step 5: Implementing the vision
Step 6: Dealing with opposition
Step 7: Making course corrections

Step 8

Evaluating the Results

The book of Nehemiah divides neatly into two parts. Chapters one through five describe the rebuilding of the wall. From these chapters we learn the process of vision. Chapters six through thirteen describe the finished product. From these chapters we learn the results of vision. It is worth noting that the results of Nehemiah's project are so dramatic that they take almost twice as much time to describe as the project itself.

The old saying is that the proof is in the pudding. The proof that God's vision is being followed and implemented is really quite obvious—because the results are dramatic.

Eight key evidences that vision has caught on

1. Completion of the vision

One of the proofs that God was in Nehemiah's work was the completion of the wall:

So the wall was completed on the twenty-fifth of Elul, in fifty-two days.
                                                        Nehemiah 6:15

One of the proofs that God is at work in His church is the completion of the vision. A half-completed vision is not the goal. A completed transition is the goal. We serve a God who majors in follow-through and completion. Paul said it this way:

being confident of this, that he who began a good work in you will carry it on to completion until the day of Christ Jesus.
                                                        Philippians 1:6

Remember God's response after He created the world:

God saw all that he had made, and it was very good.... Thus the heavens and the earth were completed in all their vast array. By the seventh day God had finished the work he had been doing; so on the seventh day he rested from all his work.
                                                        Genesis 1:31–2:2

God did not rest until the world was completed. God does not quit working on us until we are completed. God does not quit working on His vision for His church until it is completed. He is a Finisher.

> **Don't stop half-way home! You don't get any credit for runners left on base.**

The logic goes like this:

- if God gives us His vision for the church
- and if God is faithful to do His part to complete the vision
- then we should be faithful to do our part to complete the vision.

Don't stop half-way home! You don't get any credit for runners left on base.

2. Obvious demonstration of God's work

The completing of the wall had an obvious and immediate effect on all who saw it.

When all our enemies heard about this and all the surrounding nations saw it, our enemies lost their self-confidence, because they realized that this work had been done with the help of God.
Nehemiah 6:16

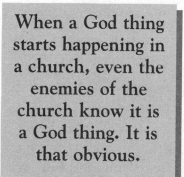

When a God thing starts happening in a church, even the enemies of the church know it is a God thing. It is that obvious.

When a God thing starts happening in a church, even the enemies of the church know it is a God thing. It is that obvious.

When a vision is working, it is obvious that God is the One at work because there is no other possible explanation other than God. When God's vision is followed, the only explanation is "It's a God thing."

Flamingo Road Church has seen God do some pretty amazing things over the past nine years. He has grown us:

- by an average of 24 percent each year
- from 300 to 2100 in worship attendance
- by starting sixteen missions and grand missions
- from 10 percent growth by reaching unchurched people to 60 percent
- from under giving budget 10 percent to over giving budget 26 percent
- through nine major transitions

This church is a long way from perfect (believe me, I know

the pastors very well). This church is a long way from finished, but there are some obvious indications that God is at work here. The answer that I give when I am asked, "How did all of this come to pass?" is always the same: "It's a God thing!"

3. Continued opposition and criticism

This one surprised me. I thought by this time that the criticism and opposition to Nehemiah's project would have stopped. Not so. Even as the wall is being finished, the critics are still at it. In fact, the accusations are more outrageous than ever:

> *"you and the Jews are planning to revolt ... and you are about to become their king."*   *Nehemiah 6:6b*

They accused Nehemiah of planning to revolt and crown himself king, and they promised to send this false report back to the king of Babylon. They even went as far as to hire spies and false prophets and plant them in Nehemiah's camp in order to try to mislead and intimidate him:

> *I realized that God had not sent him, but that he had prophesied against me because Tobiah and Sanballat had hired him. He had been hired to intimidate me ... and to give me a bad name to discredit me.*   *Nehemiah 6:12–13*

Nehemiah had widespread opposition and criticism as he began his vision—and that was to be expected. He also had opposition and criticism throughout the project—and that is not surprising. Yet it is amazing to me that even when he had finished the project, which even his enemies acknowledge was done with God's help, he was still dealing with opposition and criticism. You would think by now that the criticism would stop. The reality is this: it never does.

Two cautions concerning opposition and criticism

Concerning opposition: the only person with no opposition is the person who is doing nothing worth opposing. Opposition is at least evidence that there is something going on worth opposing.

Concerning criticism: the most blessed ministries in any arena are also the most criticized. Being criticized does not mean you will be blessed; being blessed does mean you will be criticized.

> **The only person with no opposition is the person who is doing nothing worth opposing. The most blessed ministries in any arena are also the most criticized.**

If you are not seeing any opposition and not getting any criticism, then God is not at work. The enemy always opposes and criticizes what God is blessing—even when transitions have been made and vision has been followed.

4. Emergence of new leaders

After Nehemiah built the wall, new leaders stepped forward.

> *After the wall had been built and I had set the doors in place, the gatekeepers and the singers and the Levites were appointed.*
> *Nehemiah 7:1*

Jerusalem had not needed gatekeepers or singers or priests for the temple in seventy years. Those leaders had been captured and taken to Babylon in the time of exile. The remnant in Jerusalem had not needed replacement gatekeepers because there were no gates to keep. They had not needed singers or priests for worship because the city had been destroyed.

None of these leaders for worship had been available when Nehemiah began his project. But now that the vision is complete, the leaders step forward.

What God plans, God resources

> **If you build it ...
> they will come.
> If you build
> vision, God will
> send you the
> leaders you need
> to accomplish
> that vision.**

If you wait until you have adequate leadership for the task, you will never complete the vision. If you get on the task God has for you, He will supply the leaders—because God resources what He plans. If you build it ... they will come. If you build vision, God will send you the leaders you need to accomplish that vision.

God often waits for us to take the first step of faith before He unleashes His power. Joshua had the challenge of leading his people across the Jordan into the promised land while the river was uncrossable.

So when the people broke camp to cross the Jordan, the priests carrying the ark of the covenant went ahead of them. Now the Jordan is at flood stage all during harvest. Yet as soon as the priests who carried the ark reached the Jordan and their feet touched the water's edge, the water from upstream stopped flowing. It piled up in a heap a great distance away.... The priests who carried the ark of the covenant of the Lord stood firm on dry ground in the middle of the Jordan, while all Israel passed by until the whole nation had completed the crossing on dry ground.   Joshua 3:14–17

> God often parts the waters only when we step away from the safety of the shore into the river of vision.

God did nothing about the flooded river until the leaders of the people put their feet in the water. Then and only then did He act on their behalf by parting the waters. God often parts the waters only when we step away from the safety of the shore into the river of vision.

When we first started toward contemporary music in our worship services, we did not have the musicians to pull it off. But as we started, God sent them. As we moved into contemporary music, musicians started coming out of the woodwork. The first contemporary musician we added was a drummer. Then later, we found a bass player and a guitar player. We moved from piano and organ to synthesizer as God brought other musicians. Soon there was a trumpet, and later a whole brass section. The musicians we needed trickled in one at a time, not in a flood. Today, we have three complete bands— two that rotate on the weekends and one that plays for the midweek service. We have enough singers for three complete praise teams. None of them are paid except for the two worship leaders on our staff.

If we had waited until we had the musicians to pull it off, we would still be waiting. God has resourced us as we have moved forward. If He gave us all the resources on the front end, that would not require any faith at all. He provides along the way. What God plans, God resources—not all at once, but as those resources are needed.

5. Major contributions by the people

When you first get to chapter seven of Nehemiah, it is almost an emotional letdown. The first five chapters have been action packed as Nehemiah enacts his vision. Chapter six is a nice bow on the package as the wall is officially completed. Then you get to chapter seven wondering "What's next?" It is a list. You know, a list—like the begats in Genesis and in Matthew and Luke. At first it is a list of the returning exiles, but as you read on through the rest of the chapter, it is also a list of the people who worked on the wall and all that they gave.

The impressive thing is that it shows that when vision catches on, people will contribute. Chapter seven lists some major gifts and who gave them. A few more gifts are mentioned along the way. By the end of chapter twelve the people are giving in record-setting ways:

> **When vision catches on, people will contribute.**

> *So in the days of Zerubbabel and Nehemiah, all Israel contributed the daily portions for the singers and the gatekeepers. They also set aside the portion for the other Levites, and the Levites set aside the portion for the descendants of Aaron.*
> *Nehemiah 12:47*

Don't rush by that! The same people who, in chapter five, complained that they did not have food to eat or money to pay their taxes, are now giving in record-setting ways. They are again giving the daily portions for the singers and the gatekeepers—which had not been collected in seventy years. They are now giving the

> **When vision is clearly defined and people are fully on board, giving is not a problem.**

offerings for the other Levites who are serving them—which had not been collected in seventy years. They even decide to start giving again the offerings for all the descendants of Aaron—which had not been collected in hundreds of years. These people are into giving!

In case there is any doubt left about their commitment to give, chapter thirteen tells us that the entire nation—not just Jerusalem—is giving as well:

> *All Judah brought the tithes of grain, new wine and oil into the storeroom.*   Nehemiah 13:12

What people will give to

- **People will give to vision above anything else.** Churches do not have financial problems; they have vision problems. When vision is clearly defined and people are fully on board, giving is not a problem.

- **People will give to need only if it is well expressed.** When they understand the need, most people will respond.

- **People will give to a budget rarely, if at all.** No one is motivated to give to meet the church budget when their own budget is in trouble. All that is accomplished by printing how far you are behind in a bulletin or a newsletter is the proclamation that you are failing financially.

When we first began to make our transitions at Flamingo Road, our finances went from OK to horrible. People were not buying in—literally. They were showing their lack of support in their lack of giving. The vision was not their vision and their giving was proving it. Here is how our financial journey has gone during our years of transition:

- **Year one** – As we were preparing for vision quietly behind the scenes, giving was standard, which historically had meant that we were under the budget about 10 percent to 12 percent.
- **Year two** – As we began to aggressively share our vision and discuss and plan changes, the giving plunged—the staff took voluntary 10 percent salary cuts across the board.
- **Year three** – As the vision caught on, finances began to improve—salaries were restored.
- **Year four** – Our financial recovery continued, with the church almost giving budget.
- **Year five** – We met budget for the first time in the history of the church with a 6 percent surplus.
- **Year six** – We over gave the budget 16 percent—another record high.
- **Year seven** – We were above budget 22 percent—another record.
- **Year eight** – We over gave the budget 26 percent—four years in a row of record giving.

What will the future bring? It looks good so far. People give to vision. As they own the vision, they give to the vision.

> **People give to vision.**

6. Renewed commitment to worship and obedience

Chapters eight, nine, and ten of Nehemiah are remarkable passages of Scripture. They describe the renewal of the people that results from their commitment to God's vision. This renewed commitment is seen in three ways.

• Chapter eight tells us that they *read the book of the law* together:

> *They told Ezra the priest to bring out the Book of the Law of Moses, which the Lord commanded for Israel ... He read it aloud from daybreak till noon.*
>
> *Nehemiah 8:1b, 3a*

> *Day after day ... Ezra read from the book of the law.*
>
> *Nehemiah 8:18a*

This was a big event. They built a special platform for Ezra to stand on so they could see and hear him as he read. The other leaders stood with him on the platform. For a solid week, all the people of the city of Jerusalem stood from daybreak until noon and listened as Ezra read the books of the law—Genesis, Exodus, Leviticus (I might have slept in that day), Numbers, and Deuteronomy.

• In chapter nine, the people practice *public confession.*

> *On the twenty-fourth day of the same month, the Israelites gathered together, fasting and wearing sackcloth.... They stood in their places and confessed their sins and the wickedness of their fathers. They stood where they were and read from the Book of the Law of the Lord their God for a fourth of the day, and spent another fourth in confession and in worshiping the Lord their God.*
>
> *Nehemiah 9:1–3*

Don't miss that. There is such a spirit of renewal taking

place that after they read the scripture for hours, they stayed even longer to confess their sins publicly and worship.

- They also *make a covenant with God.* They are so serious about their commitment that they put it in writing:

  "In view of all of this, we are making a binding agreement, putting it in writing, and our leaders, our Levites and our priests are affixing their seals to it."   Nehemiah 9:38

Vision produces a new commitment.

Chapter ten gives us the list of all the leaders of the people who sign this covenant with God.

Vision produces a new commitment.

A quick (or maybe not so quick) sidebar: seeker oriented churches are sometimes labeled as shallow churches. My observations as a student of church growth and church health would be these:

- **Seeker driven churches** can tend to become shallow because they are centered only on reaching seekers. If all you do is reach seekers and you do not develop them, then by default you become a shallow church. Some of the seeker driven churches have built great seeker services, but have overlooked the importance of a believer's service and of small groups to develop the new Christian into maturity.

  If all you do is reach seekers and you do not develop them, then by default you become a shallow church.

Here at Flamingo Road we are seeker sensitive—not seeker driven. We believe you can do worship and evangelism in the

> **It is the content of the gospel that is sacred, not the container in which it is delivered.**

same service. Our weekend services are definitely designed for Christians, but with the seeker also in mind. We worship; we just do it in a way that makes sense to seekers.

- **Program driven churches** tend to become shallow because they get easily sidetracked into tradition and legalism. Any time a program or method becomes the unchallenged standard, the drift in effectiveness is inevitably downward. When methods become sacred they are rarely, if ever, truly evaluated. They become ecclesiastical ruts. This is the trap of tradition. It can cause us to confuse the sacred message with the temporal method. Soon we forget that it is the content of the gospel that is sacred, not the container in which it is delivered.

It must be said that tradition is not a bad word. A tradition is a one-time creative method that worked so well that it became the standard method of operation. For example, hymns are a tradition in many of our churches today. Yet when hymns were first written, they were

rejected by many because they consisted of spiritual words put to the common tunes of the day. (Both Calvin and Luther hired secular song writers to take the popular bar tunes of the

> **A tradition is a one-time creative method that worked so well that it became the standard method of operation.**

day and put their lyrics to them.) When those hymns were later collected and put into a book of songs called a hymnal, they were again rejected by many who claimed that you could not worship God from the heart if you were singing from a

> **Any church that makes its programs, traditions, and methods into standards which cannot be challenged, evaluated, or replaced, runs the risk of falling into legalism.**

book. (I guess they were not aware that Psalms is a collection of the songs of the Hebrews—which makes it one of the first hymnals.) Hymnal burnings were commonplace in those days, but both the hymnals and the hymns eventually caught on. The radical, new method became the accepted, old tradition. Today the same debate is being waged about choruses and praise songs.

Any church that makes its programs, traditions, and methods into standards which cannot be challenged, evaluated, or replaced, runs the risk of falling into legalism. While legalism may look like the real thing, it is actually one of the most shallow expressions of Christianity in the world today.

• **Purpose driven churches** tend to become more balanced because they discover and implement God's plan for the church. They often escape the shallowness that can occur in churches that are totally seeker driven. They also avoid the trap of tradition and legalism that often accompanies being program driven. If the purpose driven church continues to reinvent and redefine itself by the constant pursuit of God and His vision for the church, balance is the result. Far from being shallow, such churches are, in fact, moving quickly toward being biblically functioning communities.

> **If the purpose driven church continues to reinvent and redefine itself by the constant pursuit of God and His vision for the church, balance is the result.**

When vision is fully pursued, the results are a renewed commitment to the Bible, to confession and repentance, and to a covenant-oriented relationship to God.

7. New people joining in

Chapters eleven and twelve document the vast numbers of people who move into the newly walled city of Jerusalem.

> *Now the leaders of the people settled in Jerusalem, and the rest of the people cast lots to bring one out of every ten to live in Jerusalem, the holy city, while the remaining nine were to stay in their own towns.*   Nehemiah 11:1

> **Vision always attracts other people.**

There was such excitement about the new vision that they held a lottery to determine who could move into the city. Wouldn't we all like to have such huge crowds wanting to get in that we had to hold a lottery in order to decide who could come to church?

Vision always attracts other people. That is because people are drawn to churches that are passionate about what they are doing and that know where they are going. People will flock to churches where God is obviously at work.

8. Openness to further change

Chapter thirteen is a remarkable conclusion to the story of Nehemiah. After taking the first five chapters to accomplish the vision and the next seven chapters to report the results, chapter thirteen basically says "and Nehemiah introduced many other changes and reforms."

A completed vision leads to openness to further change. Why? Because you have a proven track record, and a proven track record leads to trust.

> **A completed vision leads to openness to further change.**

Cutting edge churches are always in change mode. Change is a normal part of healthy living. Every living organism goes through change. Change is also a normal part of church life. Every growing church goes through change.

> **Cutting edge churches are always in change mode.**

Purpose driven churches are no longer afraid of change. They have shifted the focus from "Can we make this transition?" to "Which transition do we need to make next?"

Wrap up

When vision has caught on in a church the evidence is clearly visible. The transitions are being completed with an obvious demonstration that God is at work. Although there is continued opposition and criticism, there are also new leaders emerging. The people of the church are contributing to the work and are growing in their commitment to worship and obedience. There are new people coming to the church, being drawn by the vision of what God is doing there, and there is a growing openness to further change.

Key Truth: Give God all the credit and the glory for what has taken place.

Nothing shuts down the work of God in His church like us taking credit for what He has done. Godliness and arrogance cannot coexist in the same church leader. The spirit of godliness and the spirit of arrogance cannot coexist in the same church. When we take credit, God takes His hand off of what He has been blessing. He refuses to share His glory with anyone.

> **When we take credit, God takes His hand off of what He has been blessing.**

John the Baptist had it figured out a long time ago when he said of Jesus *"He must increase, but I must decrease"* (*John 3:30, KJV*). I believe that pride is a major problem in many of our churches and many of our church leaders. We are proud because we are focused on the good old glory days of the church in the past. We pat ourselves on the back for our doctrinal soundness. We even fool ourselves into believing that the reason our church is small is because few want to pay the price to really follow Christ. All of these are pride that is focused on ourselves rather than on the cross.

Dwight L. Moody once said, "The world has yet to see what God can do through one man that is fully committed to Him." My version of that would be "The world has yet to see what God can do through one church that is humbly and fully committed to what God wants to do."

> "The world has yet to see what God can do through one man that is fully committed to Him."

I am not impressed with me; I know myself too well. I am not impressed with the other pastors that I serve with on our staff; although they are among the best of the best. I am not even that impressed with the people of our church, although they are the most flexible church I have ever known. I am, however, very impressed with God. I am impressed with what He has done and continues to do in His church.

As long as we stay impressed with God and unimpressed with ourselves, He will continue to do impressive things in our midst.

Concluding Thoughts

Two small towns in southern Oklahoma played a big part in my growing up. After I left them, I did not revisit for several years. When I did return, I made an interesting discovery. One of those towns had changed very little. It was much as I remembered it as a child, with one exception. It was dying. Businesses were closed, school buildings unused, houses vacant. This town had refused to change with the times and as a result was dying out one piece—one person—at a time. My visit to the second town was a different experience. The old downtown area had closed down, but new malls and strip shopping centers had opened. New businesses had moved in and new schools were being built. Many of the old timers were still there, but many newcomers were also present. This town was thriving and growing.

The first town had refused to change and in so doing had pronounced its own death sentence. The second town was willing to transition and will live at least until the next needed change comes along.

I believe with all my heart that the church is running out of chances. We must now choose. If we refuse to transition, we are in fact pronouncing our own death sentence. That death will not be immediate—but it will be inevitable. On the other hand, if we embrace transition and learn the process of vision, we will not only live, we will thrive.

This book is more than just an outline for making transitions. It is a process for vision. If a church learns to make a specific transition, then we are only in the clear until the next required transition comes along. If we as church leaders learn the process of vision—the principles by which all transitions are made—then we will be prepared for whatever the future holds.

I hope that you have caught the process of vision. I pray that the principles of transition will catch on in your soul. They are big principles that can be life and church changing.

In conclusion, I offer these five statements about the process of vision as food for thought.

1. The process of vision is cyclical

> Becoming purpose driven is not a one time event; it is a way of doing church.

It is hard for most of us in the Americas to think in cyclical terms because Western thinking tends to be linear. We want to know the steps to get from point A to point B. We think of the journey between those points as being a straight line. That may be true on a football field, but it is not true in church life. Vision is not linear. It is cyclical. It is a process, not a product. The journey is as important as arriving at the destination because it is a journey you will make again and again. Becoming purpose driven is not a one-time event; it is a way of doing church. The process of vision must cycle and recycle.

The easiest way to think of the eight steps of this vision process is in a circle rather than a line.

Vision Cycle

1. Prepare for Vision

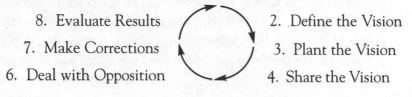

8. Evaluate Results   2. Define the Vision

7. Make Corrections   3. Plant the Vision

6. Deal with Opposition   4. Share the Vision

5. Implement the Vision

Make one change at a time. Take that change all the way through the cycle. Then restart the cycle with the next change.

2. The process of vision is continual

You never graduate from the school of vision. God always has something fresh and new to do in you and through you.

> *"Do not remember the former things, nor consider the things of old. Behold, I will do a new thing, now it shall spring forth; shall you not know it? I will even make a road in the wilderness and rivers in the desert."*   Isaiah 43:18–19

God is always doing something new and fresh and exciting in our lives and in our churches when we allow Him to do so.

> One of the dangers in seeing God's vision take root in the church is that we again settle in and get content.

One of the dangers in seeing God's vision take root in the church is that we again settle in and get content. We must always keep seeking and keep visioning.

Not that I have already obtained all this, or have already been made perfect, but I press on to take hold of that for which Christ Jesus took hold of me. Brothers, I do not consider myself yet to have taken hold of it. But one thing I do: Forgetting what is behind and straining toward what is ahead, I press on toward the goal to win the prize for which God has called me heavenward in Christ Jesus.   *Philippians 3:12–14*

Paul would certainly qualify as a mature Christian and as a man of vision. Yet he clearly states that he must keep forgetting what is behind, stretching for what is ahead, and pressing on for all that God has. Regardless of how much we have seen God do, there is more just ahead.

3. The process of vision is personal

I have centered the focus of this book on the results of vision in the church. I must emphasize that, in my experience, the greatest change will not be in the church—although those changes will be major if God's vision is fully realized. The greatest change in the vision process will be in the heart and life of the visionary. The greatest change will be in you.

The greatest change in the book of Nehemiah is in Nehemiah himself. He spent twenty years as the cupbearer to the king—which meant that he tasted and served the king's wine. That

> **The biggest change of all is in the person through whom God works to bring about His vision.**

is not exactly a high profile leadership position. Then in a few months time he becomes the governor of Jerusalem, the bearer of God's vision and one of the leaders of the Jewish return from exile. What a change! It does not matter whether it is Peter, Paul, the disciples, or any of the major leaders of God's work. The biggest change of all is in the person through whom God works to bring about His vision.

If you join God in the vision process He has for your church, the greatest change will be in you. You will never be the same. And you will be hooked for the rest of your life.

4. The process of vision is contagious

Once you become a carrier of God's vision, you will infect those around you as well. Nehemiah is the first one consumed with God's plan; but soon the officials, the priests, the

> **Once you become a carrier of God's vision, you will infect those around you as well.**

nobles, and the other leaders catch it as well. They help pass it on to the people of Jerusalem. Soon most of the city has joined in. Not everyone can catch the vision (Sanballat and Tobiah never did catch it from Nehemiah; Judas never caught it from Jesus). But most can and will.

When God captures your heart with His vision, He will use you to capture the hearts of others as well.

5. The process of vision is universal

The process of vision that is detailed in this book is meant to be applied in church settings, but it should be pointed out that it can be applied in other settings as well. Nehemiah's original application of this process was in a municipal setting. At Flamingo Road we have obviously applied it in a church setting. It can be applied in corporate, family, and personal settings as well. I have been using this process in my personal and family decisions for some time, applying it in my personal habits and goals. One of the major banks in our area is using these steps to train new employees.

God's principles work in any setting because they are God's principles. Put them to work in your context and watch God bless them.

Last thought

My hope is that you have caught the process of vision. If you have caught the process, God will use it to bring about change, both in you and through you. My bigger hope is that you will use these principles as tools of transition in your church. Many churches are applying these principles of transition to help them make the journey to being purpose driven. My greatest hope is that you will teach it and share it with others as well. That which we know well enough to teach and share is that which we know best.

May God bless you and your church as you walk hand in hand with Him on your journey through transition. The promised land of becoming a purpose driven church awaits you.

TRANSITIONING
Leading Your Church Through Change

WORKBOOK

Dan Southerland

Introduction
to the Workbook

In an effort to make using this material as practical as possible, I have included a workbook for you to use in discussing this book as a leadership team. It is the same basic outline we use in our conference on transition here at Flamingo Road Church. It is a fill-in-the-blank outline that is designed to be used in three ways:

- As a self-study tool that can be filled in after reading each chapter from the book.

- As a group-study tool that can be filled in while studying the material from the book.

- As a self-study or group-study tool that can be filled in as you listen to the audio tapes of the conference (available from Flamingo Road Church).

You have permission to reproduce any of the outlines and materials in this workbook section only for use in your local church. The workbook section is included in this book with the hope that you will copy it and use it in your church setting.

Step 1:
Preparing for Vision

No eye has seen, no ear has heard, no mind has conceived what God has prepared for those who love him.   *1 Corinthians 2:9*

What is vision? Vision is a picture of _____ _____
_____ _____ _____ in His church

The process of vision is the process of _____
_____.

"Where there is no vision, the people perish."
                                                    Proverbs 29:18

    modern: "Where there is no vision, ...

    present tense: "Where there is no visioning, ...

Rick Warren opens his book *The Purpose Driven Church* with an analogy about spiritual surfing.

    The three parts of spiritual surfing are:

    1. _____of what God is doing.

2. _____of what God is doing.

3. _____of what God is doing.

If vision is a picture of what God wants to do in His church and if the key to vision is joining God in what He wants to do and if God wants to give us His vision

then

when we are _____ **for vision,**
God gives it to us!

The Steps of Preparation for Vision

1. Collect _____

The words of Nehemiah son of Hacaliah: In the month of Kislev in the twentieth year, while I was in the citadel of Susa, Hanani, one of my brothers, came from Judah with some other men, and **I questioned them about the Jewish remnant that survived the exile, and also about Jerusalem.** *They said to me, "Those who survived the exile and are back in the province are in great trouble and disgrace. The wall of Jerusalem is broken down, and its gates have been burned with fire."*   Nehemiah 1:1–3

Nehemiah questioned those with firsthand experience about the conditions in Jerusalem.

He gathered all the information he could.

He studied the circumstance.

Vision is best birthed out of thorough _____.

Translation: it is OK to use your _____.

Two areas to go to school on:

- the _____ people in your community

- the _____ that are reaching unchurched people

2. _____ **with the status quo**

When I heard these things, I sat down and wept.
Nehemiah 1:4a

Nehemiah was heartbroken.

The walls had been down for years, but all of a sudden he experiences a holy discontent with that fact.

Vision is usually birthed out of _____ and _____.

How many times did ...

- Jesus weep over the lost sheep of Israel (Matt. 10:6)

- Moses stand in the gap for the Israelites (Ex. 17:4)

- Jeremiah weep over the burden he carried (Jer. 3:21)

As long as we are content with the status quo, we will not discover God's vision.

Vision often comes in times of _____.

3. _____

For some days I mourned and fasted and prayed before the God of heaven.   Nehemiah 1:4b

Nehemiah fasted for several days.

Jesus fasted regularly—including a forty-day fast at the start of his ministry (Matthew 4:2) and shorter fasts before major events.

A definition of fasting: giving up _____ or some other _____ in order to devote more _____ and _____ to prayer.

**Vision is usually birthed out of a _____
_____ for God's direction.**

How can we claim we are seriously searching for God's plan when we have not fasted to seek God?

4. _____

Then I said: "O LORD, God of heaven, the great and awesome God, who keeps his covenant of love with those who love him and obey his commands, let your ear be attentive and your eyes open to hear the prayer your servant is praying before you day and night for your servants, the people of Israel. I confess the sins we Israelites, including myself and my father's house, have committed against you."   Nehemiah 1:5–6

Nehemiah fasted for several days—but he prayed for several months.

He bathed his vision in prayer from start to finish.

Notice how he ended his prayer:

"O Lord, let your ear be attentive to the prayer of this your servant and to the prayer of your servants who delight in revering your name. Give your servant success today by granting him favor in the presence of this man."
                                Nehemiah 1:7

One problem we have with receiving God's vision is _____ God's voice.

Those who talk with God most usually _____
_____ _____.

Notice the progression in the promise of Jeremiah 29:11–13:

- verse 11 promises that God has a plan—a vision—for us

  "For I know the plans I have for you," declares the LORD, "plans to prosper you and not to harm you, plans to give you hope and a future."

- verse 12 tells us the way we find that vision is in prayer

  "Then you will call upon me and come and pray to me, and I will listen to you."

- verse 13 says we find God when we seek him wholeheartedly

  "You will seek me and find me when you seek me with all your heart."

Vision is usually given to those who pray _____ they get it!

If prayer is not the octane that fuels your vision, your vision will stall out and your church will be motionless.

5. _____

Notice the behind the scenes waiting going on in Nehemiah's vision:

- the wall in Jerusalem has been down for seventy years

- Nehemiah had been in the king's service for twenty years

- there is a four month time lapse between chapters 1 and 2

    "Kislev" (1:1) is the Persian name for December
    "Nisan" (2:1) is the Persian name for April

What did Nehemiah do between December and April? He waited!

Vision is usually given to those who _____ wait for it.

A working definition of God's will:

- doing the right _____
- in the right _____
- for the right _____
- at the right _____

Key #1: Rushed preparation results in _____ vision.

Our transition time at Flamingo Road:

- year one—we studied, talked, prayed and waited
- year two—we taught and shared the vision
- years three and four—we made our transitions

We took 4 years to make our transitions.

You must go _____ if you want to stay _____.

More food for thought on "Preparing for Vision"

Of the five steps of preparation: collecting information, holy discontent, fasting, prayer, waiting:

1. Which step has been the strongest in your preparation for transition?

2. Which step has been the weakest in your preparation for transition?

3. Which step has been rushed in your preparation for transition?

4. Record any other insights gained about preparing for vision.

Step 2:
Defining the Vision

Many are the plans in a man's heart, but it is the Lord's purpose that prevails.   *Proverbs 19:21*

Something dramatic happens to Nehemiah in the four month time lapse between chapters one and two.

He moves from preparing for vision to defining a very specific vision.

We must do the same.

When God leads us, He gives us _____ leadership.

Those specifics would include:

* • _____ He wants us to do

* • _____ He wants us to do it

* • _____ He wants us to do it

The Steps to Defining Vision

1. Discover your _____.

The major question we must ask here is: _____
_____?

There are _____ churches in America.

God has a specific purpose for each one of them.

If you cannot state the purpose of your church in a single sentence statement, you have not yet discovered your purpose.

Characteristics of a good purpose statement:

• it is _____

    hint: your purpose statement should fit within the parameters of the _____ _____

• it is _____

    your audience is your church—not a group of theologians

• it is _____

    it must be easily passed from one person to the next

• it is _____

   the goal is to be able to remember it, not to have to read it

K.I.S.S.S.S. = keep it scriptural, simple, sharable, and short!

2. Define your _____.

   The right questions we must ask here are:

   • Who is our immediate community?

   • Who is our primary target?

   • Who has God put in this community that we are best equipped to reach?

The wrong questions to ask here are:

   • Who do we want to reach?

   This question is too _____ and forgets that God *"does not want anyone to perish, but everyone to come to repentance."*   *2 Peter 3:9*

   • Who are we already reaching?

This question is too _____ because it assumes you are already reaching the people you are supposed to reach.

3. Realities of Targeting:

- When you aim at nothing, you hit _____ every time.

- When you aim at everything, you hit _____ most of the time.

- When you try to reach everyone, you reach _____ most of the time.

No church reaches _____!

That is why a sovereign God has allowed 485,000 churches in America.

Each one reaches different people.

The balance in targeting:

- We should welcome and celebrate anyone who walks in our doors.

- We should also define our primary target.

Defining your target is a scriptural idea:

- Paul's target: the _____ *"I am the apostle to the Gentiles."* *(Romans 11:13)*

- Peter's target: the _____ *"I had been entrusted with the task of preaching the gospel to the Gentiles just as Peter had been to the Jews."* *(Galatians 2:7)*

- James's target: the Jews who were being _____ *"to the twelve tribes scattered among the nations."* *(James 1:1)*

- Jeremiah's target: the kings and the people of _____ *"the kings of Judah, its officials, its priests and the people of the land."* *(Jeremiah 1:18)*

- Jonah's target: the backslidden people of _____ *"Go to the great city of Nineveh, and preach against it."* *(Jonah 1:2)*

Define your target four ways:

- _____

  You won't reach many South Floridians in your ministry—unless your church is located in South Florida.

  Your immediate target in miles: _____

  Your immediate target in minutes: _____

- _____

Describe the community around you:

- age
- ethnic background
- marital status
- income

- _____

Many different cultures and subcultures can exist in the same community.

- _____

There are at least 4 spiritual target groups in every community:

- the _____ that are unchurched
- _____ that are unchurched
- _____ Christians
- _____ Christians

3. **Decide your _____.**

Most churches make two mistakes when it comes to strategy:

- they define strategy _____defining purpose and target.

- they are _____ driven rather than _____ driven in their strategy.

Several key questions must be asked:

- What process will accomplish our purpose and reach our target?

- How do we move from where we are to where we want to go?

- What must _____?

- What must not _____?

- What is the best order of _____?

Key #2: The more _____ the vision, the more_____ the results.

FLAMINGO ROAD CHURCH
FORT LAUDERDALE, FLORIDA
PURPOSE, TARGET & STRATEGY

PURPOSE: To honor God by leading people to become fully devoted followers of Jesus Christ.

TARGET: There are 750,000 people within a ten mile radius of our church. They are:

- 90 percent unchurched/dechurched—attend any church less than four times a year

- 80 percent uncommitted—never made a faith commitment to Jesus Christ
- 66 percent young adults and kids—ages birth to forty-five

Flamingo Frank is our composite target. He is thirty-four years old, unchurched, uncommitted to Christ, married with two kids, has a white-collar lifestyle and is financially strapped.

STRATEGY: FULLY DEVOTED FOLLOWERS OF CHRIST

We use a twelve-step strategy organized around a baseball diamond:

1st base = commitment to membership

- I have committed my life to Christ
- I have completed the new members class

2nd base = commitment to maturity

- I am attending a weekly small group Bible study
- I am spending daily time with God
- I am giving my financial resources to God

3rd base = commitment to ministry

- I am serving in a ministry
- I am participating in ongoing training for ministry
- I am mentoring a leader

home plate = commitment to multiplication

- I am living an authentic Christian life
- I am building relationships with unchurched
- I am sharing my faith story
- I am bringing my unchurched friends to church

More food for thought on "Defining Vision"

1. In the space provided, briefly sketch out your church's purpose, target, and strategy.

    Purpose:

    Target:

    Strategy:

2. Which of these needs more refining before you proceed with the transition process? Why?

3. Record any other insights gained about defining vision.

Step 3:
Planting the Vision

After preparing for vision ...

After defining vision ...

You must plant the vision with the _____ leaders in your church.

Warning: this step is the major fall down point for many churches.

Three Sets of Leaders Must Be Involved

1. Secure the approval of the _____

_____

There are power brokers in every church.

   • E. F. Huttons

   • opinion makers

   • formal and informal influencers

Name a few power brokers in your church setting:

For Nehemiah, his power broker was a single person—the king.

The simple reality was this: to fulfill his vision, he had to secure the approval of the king.

Nehemiah secured the king's approval for:

- the _____ plan

   "If it pleases the king and if your servant has found favor in his sight, let him send me to the city in Judah where my fathers are buried so that I can rebuild it."   Nehemiah 2:5

   any change of plans requires the approval of the power brokers

- the _____ of the plan

   Then the king, with the queen sitting beside him, asked me, "How long will your journey take, and when will you get back?" It pleased the king to send me, so I set a time.
   Nehemiah 2:6

- the _____ of the plan

   Nehemiah also shared the details concerning his journey and the resources he would need.

   "letters to the governors ... provide me safe conduct ... letter to the keeper of the king's forest ... timber to make beams ..."
   Nehemiah 2:7–8

• _____ for the plan

> *"The king had also sent army officers and cavalry with me."*
> Nehemiah 2:9b

If you secure the support of the power brokers, they will tend to back you.

If you fail to secure the support of the power brokers, they will tend to fight you.

2. **Secure the assistance of those whose _____ you will need.**

In any transition, there are key people who you will need to have on board.

These leaders may not be the power brokers whose approval you need. They are other key leaders whose help you will need—and they are equally as important as the power brokers.

For Nehemiah, there were two sets of people whose help he needed:

• the governors of the surrounding lands

> *"If it pleases the king, may I have letters to the governors of Trans-Euphrates, so that they will provide me safe conduct until I arrive in Jerusalem."*
> Nehemiah 2:7

• the keeper of the forest

"And may I have a letter to Asaph, the keeper of the king's forest, so he will give me timber to make beams?"

Nehemiah 2:8

For the church, the two sets of people whose help you will need are:

• the leaders of the territory you are going to go through

• the providers of the resources

If you do not take the time to secure the assistance of the key leaders:

• You will cause _____ for the church.

• You will cause people to _____.

• You will cause leaders to _____ the church.

• You will cause great _____ for yourself.

3. Seek the advice of your _____ _____.

Effective leaders know the value of a small vision team.

Every leader needs a small handful of leaders who can dream the dream with them.

- Jesus taught thousands, sent seventy, discipled twelve, and had three in his inner circle.

- David had an army of thousands, hundreds of select troops, thirty leaders, and three mighty men.

- Nehemiah used hundreds to build the wall, scores of leaders, and a handful for his vision team.

Principles from Nehemiah's work with his vision team

A. Choose your vision team carefully.

We do not know how Nehemiah chose his vision team. The Bible does not tell us.

Common sense would suggest the following criteria:

- _____ believers

- _____ rather than detail people

- _____ people

B. Work _____ behind the scenes.

Nehemiah led his vision team to do its work out of public view.

I set out during the night with a few men. I had not told any-one what my God had put in my heart to do for Jerusalem.
Nehemiah 2:12a

The officials did not know where I had gone or what I was doing, because as yet I had said nothing to the Jews or the priests or nobles or officials or any others who would be doing the work.
Nehemiah 2:16

The point of working behind the scenes is not to be secretive; the point is to be _____.

There is a right time and place for every one in the church to be involved in the vision.

Dreaming it must be done with a small group.

C. Survey the _____ conditions.

By night I went out ... examining the walls of Jerusalem, which had been broken down, and its gates, which had been destroyed by fire.
Nehemiah 2:13

Note: You must take an honest, objective look at what is broken down and not working.

- What is working:

- What is not working:

D. **Share your** _____ **and your** _____
   with your vision team.

> *"You see the trouble we are in: Jerusalem lies in ruins, the gates have been burned with fire. Come, let us rebuild the wall of Jerusalem, and we will no longer be in disgrace."*
>
> Nehemiah 2:17

Sharing your vision with the vision team is vital—but sharing your heart is equally important.

They need to know how you got to this point—so share with them what God is doing in your heart and life.

> *I also told them about the gracious hand of my God upon me and what the king had said to me.*   Nehemiah 1:18a

Check out the response of Nehemiah's vision team when he shared his vision and his heart:

> *They replied, "Let us start rebuilding." So they began this good work.*   Nehemiah 2:18b

If a picture is worth a thousand words, then a living model is worth a million.

Key #3: Expose your key leaders to _____
churches.

Note: Several of these "key truths" are adapted from Rick Warren's lesson entitled "Leading Your Church Through Change," which is a part of Saddleback's "Purpose Driven Church Conference."

Go to school on churches that are:

- purpose driven
- parallel ministries (similar to your own)
- in the process of making similar transitions

You became imitators of us and of the Lord ... and so you became a model to all the believers in Macedonia and Achaia ... your faith in God has become known everywhere. 1 Thessalonians 1:6–8

Paul was a model for the Thessalonians; then the Thessalonians became a model for others.

There are two ways to learn:

- from _____ experience

- from the experience of _____

In church, we need to learn both ways:

- from personal experience you must learn what God wants to do in your church

- from others we can learn some creative ways to get there

You do not have enough _____ in life to learn everything by personal experience.

More food for thought on "Planting the Vision"

1. Of the three groups of leaders mentioned in this step—
    power brokers, providers of assistance, and vision team—
    which one needs more time and attention in your setting?

2. List some specific leaders you need to bring on board in
    your vision.

3. If you have not established a vision team, list some poten-
    tial vision team leaders.

4. List some possible model churches both in your area or
    state as well as in other places that you could study.

5. Record other insights gained on planting the vision.

Step 4:
Sharing the Vision

If you have given adequate time and attention to preparing, defining, and planting the vision, by this time you are ready to share the vision with the whole church.

So far Nehemiah has only shared his vision with a few leaders.

> *The officials did not know where I had gone or what I was doing, because as yet I had said nothing to the Jews or the priests or nobles or officials or any others who would be doing the work.*   Nehemiah 2:16

So far only three groups of leaders within the church know of your vision:

- the power brokers
- those whose help you will need
- the vision team

Now it is time to share the vision with two other groups of people.

1. **Share your vision with the _____ leaders.**

Before vision is shared with the church from the pulpit, it must be shared with the remaining leaders.

Nothing devalues and alienates a leader as quickly as not knowing what is coming next before the rank and file know.

It is very difficult for leaders who do not know what is going on to support what is going on wholeheartedly.

You have to read between the lines to see that Nehemiah was careful to include all the leaders in his vision:

- in Nehemiah 2:16 he tells us clearly that the *"priests or nobles or officials or any others who would be doing the work"* did not yet know of the vision

- in Nehemiah chapter three he begins to list the priests and officials and other leaders who are heading up the work on different portions of the gates and wall

What happened in between? He got the remaining leaders on board.

It is a major mistake to not take the time to share your vision with all of your leadership team before sharing it with the rest of the church.

Leaders who first hear about changes in direction and focus from the pulpit are not likely to get on board with those changes.

If your leaders are on board before you share the vision with the whole church, they will be your _____ and will help those who are struggling with the changes to get on board.

If your leaders are not on board before you share the vision with the whole church, they will be your _____ and will lead others to _____ the changes.

Suggestion: take all of your leadership away on a vision retreat.

Advantages include:

- building unity
- giving time for questions to be answered
- letting your leadership team become owners of the vision

2. **Share your vision with the remainder of the** _____.

The success of any vision comes down to one issue: will the majority of the _____ _____ get behind it.

Now it is time to share the vision with the entire church.

As you read chapter three of Nehemiah, you come to an astonishing realization: the majority of the people are working on the wall.

The lay people caught the vision!

Key #4: Vision is both _____ **and**
_____ **; therefore it must be shared**
in multiple ways.

Ten ways to share vision include:

• preaching (suggestion: preach through _____)

• small group vision studies

• _____ statements

• vision _____

• vision _____

• _____ _____

• conferences

• _____ and _____

• one on one

• _____ ___ _____ in your own life

More food for thought on "Sharing the Vision"

1. Make a list of all leaders who have not yet been brought up to speed on the vision.

2. Make a plan to share your vision with these leaders.

3. Go back to the list of ten ways to share vision on the previous page. Make a list of those which have not been implemented in your church.

4. Record any other insights gained about sharing the vision.

Step 5:
Implementing the Vision

Now it is time to start implementing changes!

Please note:

- we are now halfway through this eight-step process

- we are just now implementing changes

- most churches spend far too _____ time in preparation and move far too _____ into making changes

Three Principles to Apply in Implementing Vision

1. **Implement your changes in a _____ order.**

   The process of becoming a vision driven church usually means there are many changes to be made.

   Very few people like change.

   Implementing all the changes at once is a sure way to derail vision.

Nehemiah was strategic in where he started.

The work crews of chapter three are all organized around the gates (see verses 1,3,6,13,14,15,28).

Nehemiah had a strategic order for his project: gates first, walls second, finishing touches last.

No one but God can give you the strategic order for your transitions.

Example: At Flamingo Road, we had to make the transitions in our purpose and our target before we could make major transitions in worship style.

2. **Put key leaders to work in a** _____
   place.

   Nehemiah knew the principle of leader visibility.

   So he put his best leaders to work first on the gates.

   At each gate he put well-known leaders (again see chapter three verses 1,3,6,13,14,15,28).

   Why put them on the gates?

   Because in a city with half-torn-down walls, all the people would come and go through the gates.

   You could not come and go from the city without seeing the leaders at work.

When the people see the leaders working, they are willing to work.

3. **Put people to work where they are** _____.

Nehemiah reasoned that most of the people would want to see the wall rebuilt.

But he knew each person would be especially interested in seeing certain portions of the wall rebuilt.

So when he asked people to rebuild the wall, where did he assign them?

He assigned them to the section of the wall closest to their house.

*Benjamin and Hasshub made repairs **in front of their house** ... Azariah made repairs **beside his house** ... the priests made repairs **each in front of his own house** ... Meshukkam made repairs **opposite his living quarters**.*
from Nehemiah 3:23–30

Put people to work where they are vested:

- in areas that align with their _____

- in areas where they are already at _____

Key #5: Build on your _____**, not on your** _____**.**

At Flamingo Road, we major on three things:

- seeker sensitive weekend worship services
- small group Bible study classes for every age group
- believer oriented midweek worship service

Most churches try to do too many things.

They end up being a mile wide and an inch deep.

Note: You must _____ _____ when implementing any changes related to vision.

Most churches make changes too fast.

Name some churches you are aware of that tried to make transitions too fast:

The speed of your transition is determined by four factors:

- The _____ you must go (farther = slower).

  Major course corrections require time.

- The _____ of the ship (bigger = slower).

  Note: God measures the size of a church by the size of its

  _____.

- The _____ of the ship (older = slower).

You can teach an old dog new tricks—but you must be really patient with the dog.

• The _____ of the leader (tougher = faster).

If you are not tough enough to take the heat, don't lead a church through transition.

More food for thought on "Implementing the Vision"

1. Make a list of the major changes that need to be made in your church.

2. Place these changes in a strategic order. (Remember that changes in purpose should be made first, target second, and strategy last.)

3. List some major leaders that need to be put in visible places of leadership as these transitions are made.

4. Based on the four factors that determine the speed of your transitions (see previous page), how quickly can your church make the needed changes.

5. Record any additional insights gained about implementing vision.

Step 6:
Dealing with Opposition

If anyone in the Old Testament should have encountered no opposition, it was Nehemiah.

He is trying to rebuild a wall that will:

- make Jerusalem a safe place for all her inhabitants
- regain a piece of Jerusalem's lost glory
- enable the people to once again worship in the temple without interruption

Everyone will be happy about Nehemiah's vision—right?

Anyone that is trying to do something for God faces opposition.

So if opposition is coming—you need a plan to deal with opposition.

Two Steps to Take to Deal with Opposition

1. _____ opposition.

    Don't be surprised when opposition comes.

The greatest difficulty with opposition is it _____ you and causes you to doubt your vision.

If you are expecting it—you will be prepared.

Nehemiah experienced five different kinds of opposition.

- Expect _____. *"the nobles would not put their shoulders to the work under their supervisors."*
  Nehemiah 3:5b

- Expect _____. *"When Sanballat heard that we were rebuilding the wall, he became angry and was greatly incensed."* *Nehemiah 4:1a*

- Expect _____. *"He ridiculed the Jews."*
  Nehemiah 4:1b

- Expect _____. *"What are those feeble Jews doing? Will they restore their wall? ... What are they building—if even a fox climbed up on it, he would break down their wall of stones."* *Nehemiah 4:2–3*

- Expect a _____. *"They all plotted together to come and fight against Jerusalem and stir up trouble against it."* *Nehemiah 4:8*

Key #6: Don't take criticism _____.

You will be criticized regardless of what you do—so you might as well be criticized for doing what God wants you to do.

Am I now trying to win the approval of men, or of God? Or am I trying to please men? If I were still trying to please men, I would not be a servant of Christ. Galatians 1:10

The reality of criticism:

- You cannot please _____.

- You cannot please _____ all the time.

- You can please _____.

2. **Keep on _____.**

The second great difficulty with opposition is it _____ and drains you.

If you get off task, the vision is offtrack.

Nehemiah kept on task in five specific ways:

- Keep on _____. *"Hear us, O our God, for we are despised. Turn their insults back on their own heads."* Nehemiah 4:4a

- Keep on _____. *"So we rebuilt the wall till all of it reached half its height, for the people worked with all their heart."* Nehemiah 4:6

- Keep on _____. "After I
  *looked things over, I stood up and said to the nobles, the offi-
  cials and the rest of the people, 'Don't be afraid of them.
  Remember the Lord, who is great and awesome, and fight for
  your brothers and sons and daughters, your wives and your
  homes.'"*   *Nehemiah 4:14*

- Keep on _____. *"The officers
  posted themselves behind all the people of Judah who were
  building the wall."*   *Nehemiah 4:16b*

- Keep _____. *"Have every man and
  helper stay inside Jerusalem at night, so they can serve us as
  guards by night and workmen by day."*   *Nehemiah 4:22*

**Key #7: Be willing to let people _____
          the church.**

The reality of ministry: people will leave you no matter what
you do.

One of the hardest parts of ministry is when people you have
poured your life into leave the church.

But when you set and stay with vision, you _____
who leaves.

More food for thought on "Dealing with Opposition"

1. Name some kinds of opposition you have already encountered.

2. Name some additional kinds of opposition you should expect as you make transitions.

3. Of the five ways you must keep on track—praying, working, encouraging, leading, watching—which ones have you tended to quit doing when opposition comes?

4. Are you willing to let people who cannot support the needed changes leave the church?

5. List other insights gained about dealing with opposition.

Step 7:
Making Course Corrections

The process of transitioning a church to a purpose driven model is a major journey.

Every major journey requires course corrections along the way.

So the challenge is to _____ as you go and make necessary changes along the way.

The only thing more painful than learning from experience is not learning from experience.

Nehemiah may have been surprised at the course corrections he had to make:

- The vision was in place.
- The wall was going up.
- The opposition had been dealt with for the moment.
- The journey was well underway and the end was in sight.

And yet exactly halfway through his vision—the rebuilding of the wall—he had to make three major course corrections.

Nehemiah's course corrections are certainly not the only possible corrections we may face as we lead transition.

But the likelihood is that we will face these course corrections and even more at some point in the transition process.

Three Major Course Corrections to Be Ready to Make

1. Care for the _____.

   Anytime a church goes through major changes, someone feels neglected.

   Neglected people usually let you know by complaining.

   > *Now the men and their wives raised a great outcry against their Jewish brothers.*   Nehemiah 5:1

   Nehemiah had three groups that were complaining:

   - the "_____" group

     > *Some were saying, "We and our sons and daughters are numerous; in order for us to eat and stay alive, we must get grain."*   Nehemiah 5:2

   - the "_____" group

     > *"Others were saying, 'We are mortgaging our fields, our vineyards and our homes to get grain during the famine.'"*   Nehemiah 5:3

   - the "_____" group

> *"Although we are of the same flesh and blood as our coun-*
> *trymen and though our sons are as good as theirs, yet we*
> *have to subject our sons and daughters to slavery."*
>
> *Nehemiah 5:5a*

Nehemiah had people who were feeling:

- left out
- overlooked
- mistreated

You probably will too!

Three Possible Responses to Complainers

First possible response: _____ **them because**
they are troublemakers who just like to complain.

This is the right response if the complaint is not legitimate
and is coming from a divisive person.

> *Warn a divisive person once, and then warn him a second*
> *time. After that, have nothing to do with him.*   *Titus 3:10*

This is the wrong response if the complaint is legitimate
and is coming from a wounded person.

Notice how different translations record Nehemiah's
response:

When I heard their outcry and these charges, I was very angry. **I pondered them in my mind.**

Nehemiah 5:6–7a (NIV)

And I became very angry when I heard their outcry and these words. **After serious thought. . .**

Nehemiah 5:6–7a (NKJ)

I was very angry when I heard this; so **after thinking about it I spoke out. . .**

Nehemiah 5:6–7a (TLB)

And I was very angry when I heard their cry and these words. **Then I consulted with myself. . .**

Nehemiah 5:6–7a (ASV)

Nehemiah was furious when he first heard their complaint.

But he was wise enough to ponder them in his mind, give them serious thought, and take his time before giving his response.

The _____ you are about a complaint, the more _____ you need to be in your response.

Second possible response to complainers:_____ them because they do not understand your vision.

There will be some people in your church who do not and perhaps cannot understand your vision.

But it is a mistake to conclude this is true of everyone who has a complaint.

Nehemiah's complainers were split into three different camps.

If he had dismissed all of them as people who would never be able to understand the vision, he would have had no one left to carry out the vision.

Don't _____ your wounded just because they are complaining. It is normal for wounded people to cry out.

> *[Nehemiah] heard their outcry and these charges.*
> *Nehemiah 5:6a*

Third possible response to complainers:_____ your care for the neglected by making a plan to provide for their needs.

Nehemiah did not just commiserate with their complaints.

When he concluded they were legitimate, he took action.

> *So I called together a large meeting to deal with them.*
> *Nehemiah 5:7b*

He corrected those who were out of line and he followed through with what he promised he would do.

And the people did as they promised.   Nehemiah 5:13b

The first course correction is to care for the neglected.

2. _____ peace.

Nehemiah had to take the time to negotiate peace among his people.

> *So I called together a large meeting to deal with them and said ... "What you are doing is not right. Shouldn't you walk in the fear of our God to avoid the reproach of our enemies?"*
> Nehemiah 5:7b,9

There is a pivotal moment in most transitions where peace must be waged.

You will likely have to stop and negotiate peace among one or more of these groups:

- Between those who _____ what is happening and those who do not.

- Between those who are _____ and those who feel neglected.

- Between the _____ _____ leaders who are resisting the changes and the _____ _____ leaders who are on board.

Nehemiah had some leaders:

- who would not work (nobles in 3:5)
- who were taking advantage of the workers (officials in 5:7)
- who were fully on board (priests working on gates in 3:1)
- who were fully against him (Sanballat and Tobiah in 4:1–3)

He had no choice but to negotiate peace.

3. _____ among the people.

Since the fall of Jerusalem, the city had been ruled by appointed governors, who lived a life of luxury:

- they stayed in the governor's mansion
- they received a huge food allowance
- they collected a large salary
- they had a big staff

The former governors collected heavy taxes to support their lifestyle.

The earlier governors—those preceding me—placed a heavy burden on the people and took forty shekels of silver from them in addition to food and wine.   Nehemiah 5:15a

And these governors lived a life far above the people of the city.

Their assistants also lorded it over the people.
                              Nehemiah 5:15b

Nehemiah had received the same appointment as these governors.

> *I was appointed to be their governor in the land of Judah.*
> *Nehemiah 5:14b*

But Nehemiah's behavior was markedly different:

• He did not take the royal food allowance.

> *neither I nor my brothers ate the food allotted to the governor.*
> *Nehemiah 5:14c*

• He _____ his table with leaders, visitors, and commoners.

> *Furthermore, a hundred and fifty Jews and officials ate at my table, as well as those who came to us from the surrounding nations.*
> *Nehemiah 5:17*

• He treated his people with _____ and with _____.

> *But the earlier governors … [and] their assistants… lorded it over the people. But out of reverence for God I did not act like that.*
> *Nehemiah 5:15*

• He cared for his people.

> *I never demanded the food allotted to the governor, because the demands were heavy on these people.*
> *Nehemiah 5:18b*

• He worked on the wall _____ his people.

> *I devoted myself to the work on this wall. All my men were assembled for the work.* Nehemiah 5:16

Nehemiah stayed among his people. He was one of them.

Two choices of leadership style when it comes to vision

• _____

Which means "from on high."

This is "lord it over them" leadership.

Even benevolent dictatorship is still dictatorship.

• _____

Which means "from within."

This is servant leadership.

This is what Jesus modeled.

The difference between a martyr and a leader is ____ steps.

A martyr is __ steps ahead of his people; a leader is __ step ahead.

Lead from within.

> **Key #8: Continually _____ people why you are changing.**

> **Key #9: _____ and _____ people for the changes they do make.**

More food for thought on "Making Course Corrections"

1. Name any groups that have felt neglected as changes have been made in your church.

2. What has been the response of church leaders to those groups that have complained? Have they been listened to and cared for?

3. Are there areas where you need to negotiate peace? Between which groups?

4. Are there any behaviors that are causing the church leaders to be separated from the people?

5. Are the people being affirmed and appreciated for the changes they are making?

6. List any other insights gained about making course corrections.

Step 8:
Evaluating the Results

Chapters one through five of Nehemiah describe the rebuilding of the wall.

From these chapters we learn the process of vision.

Chapters six through thirteen of Nehemiah describe the finished product.

From these chapters we learn the results of vision.

The old saying is that the proof is in the pudding.

The proof that God's vision has been followed and implemented is clear.

Eight Key Evidences That Vision Is Working

1. _____ **of the vision.**

   One of the proofs that God was in Nehemiah's work was the full completion of the wall.

   So the wall was completed on the twenty-fifth of Elul, in fifty-two days. Nehemiah 6:15

One of the proofs that God is at work in His church is the completion of the vision.

2. Obvious _____ of God's work.

> *When all our enemies heard about this and all the surrounding nations saw it, our enemies lost their self-confidence, because they realized that this work had been done with the help of God.*   Nehemiah 6:16

When a God thing starts happening in a church, even the enemies of the church know it is a God thing. It is that obvious.

When a vision is working it is obvious that God is the one at work.

Because there is no other explanation other than God.

3. Continued _____ and
_____.

Nehemiah had widespread opposition and criticism as he began his vision—and that was to be expected.

He also had opposition and criticism throughout the project—and that is not surprising.

But it is amazing that even when he has finished the project—that even his enemies acknowledged was done with God's help—he is still facing opposition and criticism

(see Nehemiah 6:17–19).
You would think that by now the criticism would stop.

The reality is this: _____ _____ _____.

Two Cautions Concerning Opposition and Criticism

- Concerning opposition: the only person with no opposition is the person that is doing _____ worth opposing.

- Concerning criticism: the most _____ ministries in any arena are also the most _____.

4. _____ of new leaders.

After Nehemiah built the wall, new leaders stepped forward.

After the wall had been rebuilt and I had set the doors in place, **the gatekeepers and the singers and the Levites were appointed.**   Nehemiah 7:1

Jerusalem had not needed gatekeepers or singers for the temple or Levites to lead temple worship in seventy years.

The walls had been done and the temple had been unused.

Hence there were no leaders available when the project began.

But now that the vision is complete, the leaders suddenly appear.

What God _____, God _____.

If you wait until you have adequate leadership for the task, you will never complete the vision.

If you get on the task God has for you to do, he supplies the leaders.

If you build it _____ _____ _____.

5. **Major _____ by the people.**

The seventh chapter of Nehemiah is a list.

It is a list of all the people who worked on the wall and all they gave.

The impressive thing is that it shows that when a vision catches on, people will contribute.

When Nehemiah first arrives, giving is almost nonexistent.

But as the vision catches on, giving comes alive.

By the end of chapter twelve people are giving in record setting ways.

So in the days of Zerubbabel and of Nehemiah, all Israel contributed the daily portions for the singers and gatekeepers. They also set aside the portion for the other Levites, and the Levites set aside the portion for the descendants of Aaron.
                                                    Nehemiah 12:47

And by chapter thirteen, the entire nation was giving.

All Judah brought the tithes of grain, new wine and oil into the storeroom.   *Nehemiah 13:12*

What people give to:

- people will give to _____ first when it is clearly defined

- people will give to _____ when it is well expressed

- people will give to _____ rarely if at all

6. **Renewed commitment to** _____ **and to**
   _____.

Chapter eight tells us that they read the book of the law together.

They told Ezra the priest to bring out the Book of the Law of Moses, which the Lord commanded for Israel.... He read it aloud from daybreak till noon.
                                                    Nehemiah 8:1b, 3a

Day after day ... Ezra read from the book of the law.
                                                    Nehemiah 8:18a

In chapter nine the people practice public confession.

On the twenty-fourth day of the same month, the Israelites gathered together, fasting and wearing sackcloth....They stood in their places and confessed their sins and the wickedness of their fathers. They stood where they were and read from the Book of the Law of the Lord their God for a fourth of the day, and spent another fourth in confession and in worshiping the Lord their God.   *Nehemiah 9:1–3*

At the end of chapter 9 all the people make a covenant with God.

In view of all of this, we are making a binding agreement, putting it in writing, and our leaders, our Levites and our priests are affixing their seals to it.   *Nehemiah 9:38*

And chapter ten gives us the list of the leaders of the people who signed the covenant with God.

Vision produces a new commitment.

Note: Seeker oriented churches are sometimes called shallow.

_____ driven churches tend to become shallow because they are centered only on reaching seekers.

_____ driven churches tend to become shallow because they get side tracked into tradition and legalism.

_____ driven churches tend to become balanced because they discover and implement God's plan for the church.

7. _____ _____ **joining in.**

Chapters eleven and twelve document the people who move into the newly walled city of Jerusalem.

Now the leaders of the people settled in Jerusalem, and the rest of the people cast lots to bring one out of every ten to live in Jerusalem, the holy city, while the remaining nine were to stay in their own towns.   Nehemiah 11:1

Vision always attracts other people.

Because people are drawn to people who are compassionate about what they are doing and who know where they are going.

8. _____ **to further change.**

Chapter thirteen is a remarkable conclusion to the story of Nehemiah.

- after Nehemiah took five chapters to complete the wall

- after Nehemiah took seven chapters to report the results

- chapter thirteen basically says "and Nehemiah introduced many other changes and reforms"

A completed vision leads to openness to further change.

Cutting edge churches are always in change mode.

They have created such a climate of change that they have shifted the issue:

- from "can we _____ this transition?"

- to "which change do we need to make _____?"

Key #10: Give _____ all the _____
for what has taken place.

Nothing shuts down the work of God like us taking credit.

_____ and _____ cannot coexist in the same church leader or in the same church.

When we take credit, God takes His hand off what He has been blessing.

"He must increase, but I must decrease." John 3:30 (KJV)

It is amazing what God can do when we don't care who gets the credit.

More food for thought on "Evaluating the Results"

1. Review quickly the eight evidences that vision is working from the previous pages. Which of these are present in your church?

2. Based on these eight evidences, is the transition process working in your church?

3. Is God getting all the credit for the changes that are being made and the results that are happening?

4. List any other insights gained about evaluating the results.

Concluding Thoughts

The goal is not to learn how to make a specific transition.

The goal is to master the process of vision so that any transition needed in the future can be faced with confidence.

In conclusion, consider these five statements about the process of vision.

---

1. The process of vision is _____.

Vision is a process, not a product.

Vision is a journey, not a destination.

Becoming purpose driven is not a one time event; it is a way of doing church.

Vision Cycle

1. Prepare for Vision

8. Evaluate Results   2. Define the Vision

7. Make Corrections   3. Plant the Vision

6. Deal with Opposition   4. Share the Vision

5. Implement the Vision

Make one change at a time. Take that change all the way through the cycle. Then restart the cycle with the next change.

> **2. The process of vision is _____.**

You never graduate from the school of vision.

God always has something fresh and new to do in us and through us.

> *"Do not remember the former things, nor consider the things of old. Behold, I will do a new thing, now it shall spring forth; shall you not know it? I will even make a road in the wilderness and rivers in the desert." Isaiah 43:18–19 (NKJV)*

We must always keep seeking and keep visioning.

> *Not that I have already obtained all this, or have already been made perfect, but I press on to take hold of that for which Christ Jesus took hold of me. Brothers, I do not consider myself yet to have taken hold of it. But one thing I do: Forgetting what is behind and straining toward what is ahead, I press on toward the goal to win the prize for which God has called me heavenward in Christ Jesus.*
>
> *Philippians 3:12–14*

Regardless of how much we have seen God do, there is always more just ahead.

> 3. The process of vision is _____.

The greatest change in the book of Nehemiah is in Nehemiah himself. He goes from being the server and taster of the king's wine to being the visionary leader of a nation.

If you join God in the vision process He has for your church, the greatest change will be in you. You will never be the same. And you will be hooked for the rest of your life.

> 4. The process of vision is _____.

Once you become a carrier of God's vision, you will infect those around you.

When God captures your heart with His vision, He will use you to capture the hearts of others as well.

> 5. The process of vision is _____.

It can be applied in church, corporate, family, and personal settings.

God's principles work in any setting because they are God's principles.

Put them to work in your context and watch God bless them.

Last thought

My hope is that you have caught the process of vision. If you have caught the process, God will use it to bring about change, both in you and through you.

My bigger hope is that you will use these principles as tools of transition in your church. Many churches are applying these principles of transition to help them make the journey to being purpose driven.

My greatest hope is that you will teach it and share it with others as well. That which we know well enough to teach and share is that which we know best.

May God bless you and your church as you walk hand in hand with Him on your journey through transition. The promised land of becoming a purpose driven church awaits you.